ALL ABOUT CATS

Silver Tabby American Shorthair (page 12)

ALL ABOUT CATS

The Cat Lover's Dictionary

Grace McHattie

Robinson
London

By the same author:

The Cat Maintenance Manual
The Cat Maintenance Log Book
Problem Puss
Supercat
Kitten Care for Children

ACKNOWLEDGEMENTS

I would like to thank Kenneth Bryson, MRCVS, for his comments and advice on the veterinary entries and all the breeders who shared their knowledge of their own particular cat breeds with me. Any errors are my own fault.

G. McH.

Robinson Publishing Ltd
7 Kensington Church Court
London W8 4SP

First published in paperback 1994 by Robinson Publishing Ltd

First published in Great Britain 1989 by H. F. & G. Witherby Ltd

Copyright © Grace McHattie 1989

A copy of the British Library Cataloguing in Publication
Data for this title is available from the British Library.

ISBN 1-85487-266-4

Printed and bound by Arnoldo Mondadori Editore in EC

10 9 8 7 6 5 4 3 2 1

LIST OF ILLUSTRATIONS

Silver Tabby American Shorthair *frontispiece*
Usual or Ruddy Abyssinians *page* 6
American Curls 11
American Wirehair 14
Blue Tabby Angora 15
Balinese kittens 20
Seal-Point Birman kitten 21
Bombay 25
Burmese 28
Sphynx or Canadian Hairless kittens 33
Chartreuse 37
Chinchilla 41
Blue-Point Colourpoint Persian 45
Devon Rex 48
British Shorthair 53
Blue and White Exotic Shorthair kitten 60
Ferals 67
Foreign White kittens 71
Gestation table 74
Havana 79

Introductions *page* 85
Japanese Bobtail 89
Korat 92
Blotched Blue Tabby Maine Coon 99
Brown Tabby Manx 102
Cymric 103
Brown Tabby Norwegian Forest Cat 107
Oriental Tabby 111
Red Self Persian 114
Giving pills 115
Ragdolls 123
Russian Blue 127
Tortoiseshell and White Scottish Fold 129
Seal Tabby-Point Siamese 133
Singapura 136
Snowshoe 137
Usual or Ruddy Somali 141
British Shorthair 145
Tonkinese kittens 149
Turkish Van kittens 153

PHOTOGRAPHIC ACKNOWLEDGEMENTS

Stephe Bruin: 15, 20, 21, 28, 33, 37, 45, 48, 53, 60, 67, 71, 89, 92, 99, 102, 103, 107, 115, 129, 133, 145, 149, 153

Animals Unlimited/Paddy Cutts: 41, 111, 127, 141

Marc Henrie: 114, 123

Vickie Jackson: 6, 11, 14, 79, 137

Larry Johnson: frontispiece, 25, 136

Grace McHattie: 85

Two Usual or Ruddy Abyssinians, both USA Grand Champions

A

Words in **bold** indicate other entries.
References to illustrations are given after the head word.

Abyssinian *(see opposite)*

The first known Abyssinian was brought back from Abyssinia – now called Ethiopia – in the 19th century but they are still not common cats. Their fur is 'ticked', that is, each hair has two or three bands of colour, except on the face, which has tabby markings. They are bred in a variety of colours: usual (which is apricot ticked with black giving a lion-coloured effect), sorrel (apricot ticked with brown giving a fox-coloured effect), blue (oatmeal ticked with blue), as well as fawn, chocolate, lilac, red, cream and tortoiseshell.

Abyssinians love company, human or feline, and tend to be one-person cats. A stay-at-home owner is ideal for the Abyssinian, which will repay companionship with friendliness and affection. They are highly intelligent, very active and often keen hunters. Although they enjoy using up their energy out of doors, they will settle down quite happily in a flat.

They are easy to groom, hand-stroking is often all that is required, but once-weekly combing will keep them looking their best.

accidents

When a cat is involved in an accident out of doors its first instinct is to hide. Prevent it from doing so if you can. A cat which does not want to be found, won't be, and could die from its injuries. A cat will drag itself away after an accident to a quiet, safe place until it recovers and, in the wild, this would have survival value. In domestic circumstances, a visit to the vet has much higher survival value.

Restrain the injured cat if you can. Place it in a box or carrier so that it cannot hide or, if you do not want to touch the cat, up-end a box or carrier over it. Always approach an injured cat with great care, even if it is your own – pain can make the friendliest cat bite the hand which tries to help.

If a cat struggles and no box or carrier is immediately available, immobilise the cat (without making any injuries worse) by wrapping a jacket around it, then take it to a vet. Do not give an injured cat alcohol or painkillers: these are toxic to cats. See also **bleeding**.

adoption (of a cat by a human)

Not every cat lover is able to give a home to a cat; allergy, lifestyle, or home circumstances may preclude this. However, it need not mean that the cat lover remains catless. He or she can simply 'adopt' a cat. Many rescue shelters become permanent homes to elderly or nervous cats which, like human beings in gaol, have become institutionalised and would not adjust to life outside their safe shelter.

These cats are often offered for 'adoption'. Their human adopters pay some or all of the cost of their keep but the cats remain living in the shelters. Adopters can visit their cat as often as they like. Progress reports and photographs are sometimes sent by the shelter, who might even provide a Christmas card in December!

adoption (of kittens by a cat)

Cats are wonderful mothers. They are wonderful mothers of their own kittens, other cats' kittens, puppies, gerbils and baby rats. If it moves, and it's small, and they've just had kittens, they'll mother it. Cat breeders who have several breeding females (called queens) which have had litters around the same time find that the mums will pop into their friends' nests and pinch a few extra kittens to feed if they are not being looked after at the time. These caring traits are invaluable if, as occasionally happens, a queen cannot feed her own kittens. Simply put the kittens in with a queen which has just kittened and your feeding problems are over. Breeders and those who rescue unwanted kittens swap litters around, if necessary, usually with excellent results.

I have heard of ways to persuade a queen to accept strange kittens but, in my experience, they are unnecessary. Just in case, it is recommended that some of the fostering queen's milk is expressed, then rubbed on the kittens, which should be placed in the kittening pen when the queen is absent. If the foster mum shows any sign of rejecting the kittens, remove them and repeat the operation.

There is a rumour that, in the distant mists of time, moggy kittens were skinned and their skins used to cover pedigree kittens whose mother was unable to feed them, in order for the moggy mum to accept them. If it ever happened, it was carried out by such a minority we are probably talking about one person – it simply isn't necessary to go to such lengths.

affection

Despite popular myth and legend, cats are remarkably affectionate. And it is not just cupboard love – they will love you as much at feeding time as they would when the cupboard is bare. So if your cat is not showing you affection, you are doing something wrong.

All cats have their individual ways of showing affection. Some are unmistakable – the kneading, treading, drooling, purring lapcat needs no explanation. Other cats are more restrained. Some will show affection when they are alone with their owners; only then will they climb on laps and purr and knead. They will wait until other members of the family – and other pets – are out of the way before making a fuss of their person. Some will come running when they hear their owner's car – the sound of which they will pick out from hundreds of others, rolling on the ground in an ecstasy of welcome.

Other cats will eat the food their owners provide then turn their backs but this, if you understand the cat's silent language, is revealing. The back-turning cat is saying that it is not a threat; it may be a little frightened of its owner's voice or behaviour. Modify either and it should become more friendly.

Many pedigree cat owners refer to themselves as their cats' 'mum'. This is quite an accurate description, because when a kitten leaves its real mother, it transfers its affections to its new human 'parent' and behaves towards that person in the same way it behaved towards its mother. A kitten's mother is always dominant to it and its owner later assumes that boss role. A kitten will show affection to its owner by purring; it learned to purr at the age of just a few days to let its mother know that all was well. A kitten will knead its owner's lap; it learned to knead to express its mother's milk and associates the action with a pleasurable experience – the experience of being warm, comfortable and well-fed. Some cats will lie on their backs and invite stroking of their stomachs; this is not just a sign of affection but of trust, as cats are extremely vulnerable in that position.

So are you picking up your cat's signals? If it rolls on its back, inviting a stroke, do you oblige? If it blinks, do you blink back? Learn your cat's **body language** and you can become a friend as well as an owner.

affiliation

Cat clubs exist to promote knowledge of particular breeds among those who might wish to breed them. Each club will be affiliated to a registration organisation. In the United Kingdom, this will be the **Governing Council of the Cat Fancy** or the **Cat Association of Britain**.

agouti

Colour pattern formed by bands of black, brown and yellow colour, which, by means of optical illusion, look a different colour entirely, for example, the 'grey' stripes of the **tabby**.

ailourophile

A cat lover. Famous ailourophiles include Albert Schweitzer who, although left-handed, would write with his right hand rather than disturb his cat who would sleep on his left arm, and the prophet Mohammed, who cut off his sleeve rather than wake a cat which was sleeping on it.

ailourophobe

A cat hater. Famous ailourophobes include Adolf Hitler and Napoleon who was terrified of cats and could be reduced to a quivering jelly by the presence of a small kitten.

albino

Albinism is rare in cats. A true albino cat has white fur and pinkish eyes, as the blood vessels in the eyes can be seen due to lack of pigment in the iris. Distance perception may be a problem in the albino cat, so affecting its ability to hunt.

alcohol

A liquid which is poisonous to humans in large quantities and poisonous to felines in tiny quantities. Never give a cat alcohol.

allergy (to cats)

Cat allergies can be caused by a variety of allergens: fur, **dander** on the skin, or saliva, so the quest of many cat lovers to find a 'non-allergenic cat' may be doomed to failure. Even the hairless **Sphynx** can provoke an allergic reaction in some sufferers. **Rex** cats, because of their short fur, have been hailed as the saviours of the allergic cat lover, but allergy problems have often continued. A few sufferers may find they are not allergic to Rex cats, but a large number will find they are. Desensitising injections, the raw material of which is acquired from cat combings, are available but are not suitable for everyone. Unfortunately, serious allergy of this kind has only one really effective 'cure' – don't keep a cat. A cat lover with serious allergy problems might consider adopting a cat, which they would support financially, but which would continue to live in a rescue shelter (see **adoption** of a cat).

For those with a very mild allergy, steps can be taken to minimise the problem:

▷ groom your cat daily and keep its fur in good shape with the aid of a conditioner

▷ bath your cat regularly, if it does not object too strenuously

▷ empty litter trays carefully, possibly wearing a dust mask

▷ have as many smooth, washable surfaces in the home as possible and wipe over regularly with a damp cloth

▷ an air purifier may help – especially one for commercial use.

allergy (of cats)

Cats can suffer allergies too, with symptoms as varied as conjunctivitis, sneezing, coughing, diarrhoea or bald patches. Some of their allergies can be surprising – many, for example, are allergic to milk. The lactose in milk will give them diarrhoea, so they should be given only water to drink. Some cats are allergic to their food, even manufactured foods which have no ill effect on most other cats. The allergen may be an additive in the food, or the meat itself, as a few cats are even allergic to red meat and consequently must live on chicken and fish diets.

Cat litter can cause problems too, especially if it is very dusty or if deodorants are added. Some asthmatic cats have shown an improvement when their litter medium has been changed.

Many other everyday items can cause allergic reactions in cats: carpet cleaners or other household cleansers, pollen, fleas, plas-

tic bowls – even cigarette smoke. One cat which shares its owner's bed started sneezing violently about once a fortnight. This corresponded with the nights its owner used a particular body lotion. She stopped using it and the sneezing stopped.

alone

Something you should not leave cats for long periods. See **boredom**.

alopecia

Loss of fur in patches. It can be caused by hormone imbalance, dietary deficiency or other reasons. See **bald patches**.

alter

Another word for **neutering** or spaying.

American Curl   (see opposite)

The American Curl, although not truly related, can be considered to be a cousin of the **Scottish Fold** if only because both cats are natural mutations displaying what some would consider to be deformed ears. In the American Curl, the ears curve backwards and have hairy ear tufts.

The first American Curl was a stray, turning up on a California doorstep in 1981. Two of her kittens also had unusual ears and it was discovered that the 'Curl' gene was dominant – only one parent needs to have curled ears to pass on the quality to its offspring.

American Curls should be slender cats with moderate heads and large eyes set on a slight bias. The coat should lie flat and be medium long and silky. In temperament, these cats are affectionate, placid, yet playful.

American Rex

See **Rex**.

Young American Curls, showing their unusual ears

American Shorthair *(see frontispiece)*

If the **British Shorthair** can be called the native cat of the British Isles, the American Shorthair must be the native cat of the USA, despite, or because of, its long history of shared ancestry with its British cousin. It is thought that at least one cat was on board the *Mayflower* when the Pilgrim Fathers set sail for the New World. Its function would undoubtedly have been that of official expedition rodent exterminator – for which job it would have been well qualified, if its offspring are anything to go by. For the American Shorthair is a strong, natural hunter, 'a trained athlete with all muscles rippling easily beneath the skin' according to the standard of points for the breed. It should be medium to large-sized, well developed but not **cobby**, with a large, full-cheeked head.

It is not always easy to tell the American and British Shorthairs apart and your geographical location is likely to give you the biggest clue. The British Shorthair should have a rounder face and may be slightly smaller too. But whether American or British, these are intelligent, friendly and adaptable cats.

American Wirehair *(see page 14)*

Wirehairs were given their name because of the appearance of their coat – not because of the feel of it. The coat is only slightly less soft than that of the **American Shorthair**, which resembles the American Wirehair closely. The big difference between the two breeds is the 'wired' coat.

The amount of wiring varies from cat to cat. The hairs of the coat are hooked or bent and the whiskers may be bent too. The cats can become 'unwired' when combed, because the hooked ends catch on the comb and are pulled out. So these cats are not often combed and, if bathed, should be allowed to dry naturally as hairdryers can straighten out the hair. Some cats have a lot of wiring while others have very little and the location of the wiring also varies from cat to cat; it need not be all over the body. Many Wirehairs look as if they have extremely plush, dense coats; the coats look otherwise normal.

The first Wirehair appeared as a natural mutation in a farm cat's litter and the breed can be outcrossed with **American Shorthairs** so, as might be expected, the breed is healthy and hardy.

amputation

It is surprising how many people confuse cats and racehorses. Racehorses do not manage very well on three legs, but cats adapt to an amputated limb with no trouble at all. In fact, you have probably seen a number of three-legged cats without realising they were three-legged – they can walk, run, leap and get into mischief without any slowing down at all. If a serious accident leaves one limb paralysed or damaged beyond repair, amputation will be recommended. It is not cruel, the cat will adapt well and euthanasia need not be considered.

anaemia

Anaemia may result from bacterial infections, poisons, parasites, kidney or liver disease, dietary deficiencies or loss of blood. Symptoms include loss of appetite and poor fur condition, lack of energy and unwillingness to play. The tongue and gums will look pale. Blood tests will show which of the above causes is involved and treatment may include iron supplements, probably by injection, and possibly blood transfusions in severe cases. See also **Feline Infectious Anaemia**.

anaesthetics

Cats are usually anaesthetised by intravenous injection of barbiturates. Anaesthesia is maintained with a gas or volatile liquid given through a rubber mask or a tube inserted into the windpipe (trachea). Anaesthetic is given to cats for many operations which would not require it when performed on humans, for example, teeth scaling. Cats are usually taken to a vet early in the morning of the day an operation is to be performed, having been given nothing to eat since the previous evening. It is best not to use de-fleaing products just before anaesthesia as, together, the treatments may prove toxic.

Angora   (see page 15)

If the Angora had a haircut, it would be called a **Foreign**, for it is, simply, a Foreign-type cat with long hair. As such, it is no surprise that they adore attention and admiration. They need company and are talkative cats, although the volume of their voices varies from cat to cat. They are affectionate and full of fun.

At one time, the names Angora and **Persian** were used almost as synonyms but this is not so today. The Angora has a finer coat than a Persian, with no woolly undercoat, so it does not mat and daily grooming is not necessary. The Angora moults regularly although this is not always obvious. They can have such long fur that it is sometimes spun into yarn, then knitted into garments.

The first of the new generation of Angoras turned up unexpectedly in an English litter of Foreigns after the old type of Angora had almost died out. There are a wide range of colours in the Angora, including tabby, tortoiseshell and Siamese-pattern. The Turkish Angora (which is often white and is the cat most people think of as an Angora) is recognised in the USA and Europe but not in the United Kingdom.

The Angora is also referred to as the Mandarin cat, Foreign Longhair and Oriental Longhair.

antiseptics

Probably the best antiseptic for use on a cut paw is a saline solution. Dissolve one teaspoonful of salt in one pint of warm water in a jug, then place the cat's paw in the jug. Swoosh it around for as long as your cat will let you.

Many antiseptics and disinfectants are toxic to cats, so should always be used with care. Savlon is fine, but, confusingly, not Dettol liquid, which looks much the same. Cats are unable to detoxify phenols so check labels or ask your pharmacist's advice and avoid anything which contains phenols. Carbolic and coal tars should also be avoided as they, too, are toxic.

anus

This part of the cat's anatomy is usually of little interest to anyone until something goes wrong with it. If your cat licks the area excessively, this may indicate that the anal sacs are impacted. Veterinary attention is needed to squeeze the contents out manually.

Irritation of the anal area may follow diarrhoea. If so, the area should be cleaned, dried and treated with a zinc or nappy rash ointment and the cat should not be allowed to lick this off. If you cannot prevent your cat licking off the ointment by diverting its attention by playing with it or giving treats, you may have to resort to an **Elizabethan collar**.

Always check a kitten's bottom before purchase. If there are signs of diarrhoea, don't

American Wirehair, USA Best of Breed
(page 12)

buy the kitten. If you are determined to buy the kitten, come back a few days later to check its health again. If there are still signs of diarrhoea, don't buy it. One attack of diarrhoea may be caused by the kitten eating too much, but continuing diarrhoea could be the symptom of a serious illness.

The anal glands form an important part of the scent recognition process of cats which can sometimes be seen rubbing their bottoms against vertical surfaces to mark them with their scent. Fortunately, the scent glands on the chin and mouth appear to be of more importance to cats who rub these glands against their owners in order to mark them as 'theirs'.

AOC

Any Other Colour. When the first cat shows were held there were few established breeds, so cats were classified according to their colour. For example, there would be classes for black cats and tabbys, but many more cats would find themselves lumped in the Any Other Colour category. Today, non-pedigree cats, when shown, are classified according to colour with an AOC category for the less-common colours.

AOV

Any Other Variety. Before a breed of cat is recognised by a registration body, there must be evidence that the cat will **breed true** and that a number of awards or certificates have been granted in AOV or **assessment classes** at shows. AOV will also be used at small shows to group together the few entrants which do not belong to the most numerous breeds.

Blue Tabby Angora (page 13)

appetite

The average sized adult cat requires 350 kilocalories each day – three times as many calories, weight for weight, as its owner! This equates roughly to the contents of a 400g can of cat food or about 200g of fresh, fatty meat. Low fat meats such as white fish or chicken have a lower calorific value so a cat on this type of diet will need more food.

Appetite varies throughout life from hungry kittens which should be fed four or five times a day, to the 'average' of the adult cat, to the smaller appetite of the older cat. Queens in kitten will have increased appetites and, when they are producing milk for their kittens, they may require three or four times as much food as normal.

You will learn the amount to feed your cat by trial and error. If your cat starts to put on weight or has to make six trips a day to its litter tray, you are overfeeding it and should reduce its food.

Appetite may vary temporarily. If a cat is feeling unwell, it will be disinclined to eat. It may help tempt it to eat if you liquidise a strong-smelling food, such as tuna or mackerel, with a little water or broth. In hot weather, most cats will not be interested in food. Feed them in the evening when it is cooler. See also **diet**.

Archangel cat

See **Russian Blue**.

artificial respiration

If a cat has been in water and is unconscious, check that the mouth and throat are not obstructed, hold the cat upside down by the hind legs for twenty seconds or so and shake its body several times to clear the airways of water. Then hold its mouth and lips closed and blow into its nostrils. Blow until the chest rises and then let the animal exhale. Repeat six to ten times per minute. Press the chest to expel air, if necessary.

If you don't want to give mouth-to-mouth resuscitation, lay a cat which has stopped breathing on its side, check that mouth and throat are unobstructed, and extend the head, pulling the tongue forward. Place your hand on the ribs with your other hand on top of that. Press down gently and release immediately; repeat fifteen times per minute.

If a cat's heart has stopped, place it on its side and place your hand on the middle of its chest. Press down firmly but gently for a count of two and release for a count of one. Be gentle as you could crush its ribs if you apply too much pressure. Repeat sixty times per minute, giving mouth-to-mouth resuscitation at the same time.

ash

Ash is a word you will see on the labels of commercially-prepared cat foods and it refers to the mineral content of the food. Ash is what remains when the food is burned and consists, in the form of oxides or salts, of the macro-minerals – calcium, phosphorus, magnesium, sodium and potassium – and the micro-minerals (or trace elements) required in much smaller amounts, such as iron, iodine, copper, zinc and manganese.

Asian

Asian describes a cat of **Burmese** type which does not yet have a recognised coat colour or pattern, for example the **Burmilla**, **Burmoiré** and **Bombay**. The **Tiffany** also qualifies as an Asian as it is of Burmese type but with long fur, which is not recognised yet in the Burmese.

aspirin

Never, *ever* give a cat aspirin, except on veterinary advice, and then only in the most carefully measured doses. Aspirin (acetylsalicylic acid) can kill a cat, or cause vomiting, depression and anorexia. Do not give your cat paracetamol either. If it is in pain, take it to a vet.

assessment classes

Assessment classes are those in which new, as-yet-unrecognised breeds can be entered. The cat club for the breed provides a provisional standard of points and the cats are judged according to it, receiving merits if they are up to standard. A number of merits must be collected by the club before the breed can be recognised.

awns

Awns are the sharp-pointed 'beards' of grasses and they are a blasted nuisance. If they get into your cat's ears or between its toes they can be carefully tweezered out, if found soon enough. If not, they can travel under the skin and veterinary attention is needed. Awns can also get under eyelids and swift veterinary attention is essential.

B

bad breath

Cats are carnivores and the breath of a carnivore is never entirely sweet. However, if your cat's breath smells less sweet than usual it may be a symptom of a mouth or gastric problem. An infection or gum disease (**gingivitis**) could also cause bad breath. **Tartar**, which can build up on the teeth, especially the teeth of older cats, is a common cause of bad breath. Regular cleaning of your cat's teeth can help prevent tartar buildup as can the daily addition of a few pieces of dry food to its diet. See also **teeth**.

bald patches

Bald patches can have a variety of causes. A hormone imbalance can result in large, symmetrical bald patches, often on the cat's underside and the insides of its hind legs. This is not uncommon in neutered cats and a form of feline hormone replacement therapy is used to clear up the problem in some cases. Milder cases can be left untreated at your vet's discretion, as the condition sometimes adjusts itself spontaneously.

Allergies can cause bald patches too. Bald chins are sometimes seen on cats which have an allergic reaction to their plastic feeding bowls or as a result of feline acne. Flea allergy can cause extreme itchiness and bald spots.

Ringworm, a fungal infection, will appear in a variety of guises, from a circular bald patch with raised, hard skin visible beneath to a balding patch which otherwise looks quite normal. Nutritional deficiencies, **mange** and **eczema** can all result in bald patches.

Sometimes a cat will lick an injury until a bald patch appears. Some cats will overgroom themselves through boredom, licking their fur until they lick away a patch of it. In all cases of bald patches, veterinary advice should be sought.

Balinese *(see page 20)*

The Balinese first appeared by accident in litters of **Siamese** kittens, and is basically a longhaired Siamese. The first ones were neutered and sold as pets (ie not for breeding) but when it was discovered that they bred true and retained many of the Siamese characteristics, they were developed into a separate breed.

Like the Siamese, they are affectionate and playful, but fortunately not usually as noisy as their shorthaired relatives! They are kittens for ever, enjoying attention and happiest in company when their capacity for fun and companionship can be exercised to the full.

Grooming is not difficult as there is no woolly undercoat. Their silky coat rarely mats and shedding is not heavy. Balinese can be found in the same points colour combinations as the Siamese.

bandaging

If your cat requires bandaging it probably requires veterinary attention, in which case you can let your vet apply the bandage. Your cat will be much better at removing bandages than you are at applying them. But, should you wish to try: clean any wound with a salt solution (one teaspoonful salt to one pint of warm water), place a sterile pad on the wound and bandage evenly but not too tightly and fasten with a safety pin. A little petroleum jelly on the pad will stop it sticking to the wound.

bathing a cat

First, gather all the necessary equipment in the vicinity of a sink. You will need:

▷ a cat shampoo (don't use human dandruff preparations or detergent)
▷ several towels
▷ bowls of hand-warm water
▷ a jug
▷ towelling or a rubber mat for the bottom of the sink
▷ an apron, to keep you dry
▷ a warm, draught-free room in which to place your wet cat

If your cat dislikes being bathed, trim its claws. It will still struggle, but you won't get hurt so much. If it is used to a collar or a harness, you can put it on and use it to keep a grip on the cat – don't use a flea collar.

Put on your apron and place the towelling or rubber mat in the bottom of the sink to stop your cat slipping. Pour a few centimetres of hand-warm water into the sink and mix in a few drops of shampoo. This will break the surface tension and make it much easier to wet your cat's fur right down to the skin.

Lift your cat into the sink, holding it with one hand, while you use the jug to scoop water from the sink over its fur, avoiding the face and ears. When it is thoroughly wet, lather in the shampoo, again avoiding the face and ears. Rinse thoroughly, using the bowls of warm water. Wrap your cat in a towel and dry it as much as possible. It may shake itself to get rid of excess water, so ensure you are still in a room which is easily dried. Wrap your cat in another, dry towel, and rub again. Some cats enjoy being left wrapped in another, dry towel until their fur completely dries out because, until it does, they will feel chilly. Keep your cat indoors in a warm room for the rest of the day and night.

If just the thought of the above gives you an attack of the vapours, see **dry shampoos**.

beds

You need not spend a lot of money on providing a comfortable bed for your cat. An empty cardboard box (which has held a 'clean' product, not something strong-smelling), with several layers of newspaper and a clean old blanket on top can provide warmth and comfort. Once a month, throw the bed away and make a new one. Wash the blanket to remove any flea eggs and loose fur.

Ensure that the bed is placed out of draughts, or is draught-proof, and that it is big enough to allow your cat to stretch out. Your cat will appreciate its bed being placed in a low-traffic area, where it won't be trodden on. Cats also enjoy a sense of security from sleeping in a high position, so placing your cat's bed on top of a piece of furniture would probably be welcomed.

There is a wide range of manufactured beds to cater for your cat's comfort. Modern beds are fully washable – usually machine-washable – an important hygiene consideration. The basic model is a foam-filled, circular bed with a fitted cover. On more expensive models, the cover may be fur fabric and will zip off for separate washing. Some manufacturers will cover a bed in your own fabric, so it will match the rest of your room. An 'igloo' is a bed which has a hooded top. In a household with more than one cat they will use it as an ambush point – one will hide inside it and jump out at the others.

Beanbags are hygienic, popular and extremely warm. A cat will scoop out a hollow for itself and lie in it, so that the heat is conducted all around its body by the polystyrene bead filling. Covers usually zip off for washing and the inner bag and filling can also be washed by hand. Shake off excess moisture and hang up to dry, preferably in the sun. One disadvantage of beanbags is that their filling can confuse some cats. When they scoop out their hollows, the filling sounds (and undoubtedly feels) like cat litter underfoot, so it is not surprising that many 'clean' cats urinate on their beanbags. All you can do is wash it and try again.

Don't buy a bed while your cat is a kitten. Wait until it grows up and choose one to suit its adult size. Some cats will sleep curled up but some prefer to sleep stretched out – and will need a bigger bed.

bi-colour

A cat with a coat of a solid colour with white

Balinese kittens, (left to right) Chocolate-Point, Seal-Point and Blue-Point (page 18)

Seal-Point Birman kitten (page 22); *balls of wool and thread make dangerous toys (see needles)*

patches. The white on the coats of pedigree bi-colours is required to be symmetrical and patterned as laid down in the standard of points for the breed.

birds

Bird-loving cat lovers are shocked and exasperated by their cat's refusal to see birds as anything other than fair game. But hunting is a deep-rooted instinct, and the instinct is triggered by movement. When a cat sees a small, moving bird, it can do nothing else but chase it. The fact that the cat is well fed and does not need the bird for food has nothing to do with it. It is best just to accept this part of your cat's life if you can. If the bird was a rat you'd be only too pleased at your cat's prowess.

However, if you feel you cannot live with a bird-killing cat, you could try some basic aversion therapy. Tie a few feathers to the end of a piece of string and tie the other end to a stick or cane. Have a filled water pistol handy and dangle the feathers in front of your cat. Every time the cat pounces on the feathers, squirt it with water. Cats hate getting wet and will soon associate the feathers with a soaking.

I would not give my cats such aversion therapy, nor would I 'bell' them. I don't believe cats should wear collars as there is a risk of strangulation. As for bells on collars, cats are expert at staying perfectly still for long periods while a bird comes into range. Before the bird hears the bell it is dead.

Some owners try to find a cat which has not been taught to hunt by its mother, believing it will not possess the hunting instinct. It probably will possess the hunting instinct but, with luck, it might not be any good at hunting. Many cats are not, clasping thin air with crossed paws and looking puzzled as their prey soars out of reach. However, cats which come from a long line of indoor cats – which have never had the opportunity to hunt birds or mice – often still possess a definite killer instinct, and can be seen stalking and killing wasps and flies with supreme concentration and dedication.

Birman   (see page 21)

Birmans come from Burma and are reputed to be the sacred cats of that country. Birmans were said to be temple cats and are surrounded by myth and legend. Their beautiful golden body colour with darker points and white gauntlets has a legendary beginning too. They were said to be pure white cats once but they defended the temple priests against attackers, and, as a reward, a golden goddess turned their fur to gold, with brown points to symbolise the earth, and white gloves for purity. The early Birmans came to Europe as gifts from the temple priests (and if you believe all that you'll believe anything).

Birmans have small voices and gentle ways. They are renowned for their even temperaments and are sometimes described as ideal cats for someone who would like a **Persian** but does not have time to groom a Persian. The Birman's coat is silky, so is not inclined to mat, but a short daily grooming session is essential. Shedding is minimal with a well-cared-for Birman.

Birmans are great characters and keep themselves occupied, always wanting to be 'out and doing'. They are affectionate and intelligent and enjoy cuddling. Very people-oriented, the Birman would fit in well in most households. They are devoted to their owners and may follow them around. Birman kittens are very forward and active but become quieter as they mature.

Birmans are now bred with different **points** colours, including Seal-Point and Blue-Point.

bite

A cat's 'bite' is the position of the upper and lower teeth when the mouth is closed. The incisors (the middle teeth) should meet, with the four canines neatly slotting through one another. Unfortunately, in some pedigree cats bred for flattened faces, jaw deformities have appeared, leading to **overshot** or **undershot jaws**, with imperfect bites.

bites and scratches

Cats' mouths are awash with bacteria and bites should always be treated immediately. If your cat is bitten or scratched by another cat, clean the wound with a safe **antiseptic**. Keep a close watch on the wound for the next few days for signs of infection, ie signs of discharge, redness, swelling or pain. Should the wound become infected, antibiotic treatment will be necessary and you should consult your vet immediately you notice a problem. Many cats get bitten as the result of territorial fights and entire tomcats are more likely to fight, and become injured, than neutered cats.

If a human is bitten, the wound should be immediately held under running water to 'flush' out any bacteria and antiseptic should be poured into the wound. Cat owners would be well advised to keep their anti-tetanus vaccination up-to-date; see **cat scratch fever**. Animal bites are much more serious in some parts of the world than others; see **rabies**.

biting

Few cats bite because they are truly aggressive. In some cases the 'bite' is restraining behaviour misunderstood by the owner, or it may be due to over-active playfulness.

Some cats will play with their owners one minute and will turn round and bite them the next. These are cats which become over-stimulated by play and owners should be alert for signs of mounting tension in their cat and stop playing with them before they reach the biting stage.

Play is closely associated in a cat's mind with fighting and biting, because, in kitten-hood, littermates have play-fights as practice for defending themselves against other cats in adult life. Some cats will switch over from 'play mode' to 'fighting mode' when playing with their owners, quite unable to stop them-selves. This most frequently happens when a cat's tummy is being tickled as fighting cats will scrabble away at one anothers' bellies with their feet. The owner's tickling dupli-cates this action and sets off the fighting in-stinct. For the same reason, some cats will ambush their owners, leaping out from be-hind furniture and biting their ankles. To stop this behaviour, distract the cat by tossing down a small toy and its attention should be diverted to that.

Some 'bites' are, in fact, restraining holds. A mother cat has no hands with which to hold her kittens while they are washed, so she will use her teeth instead. She will gently but firmly clamp her teeth around her kittens' necks and they will immediately go limp, then she starts to wash them. When they start to wriggle again, she grasps them in her teeth until they go limp, when she continues to wash them. Some cats will do this to their owners' hands and wrists to restrain them, so that they will stop doing whatever it is they are doing. This hold is usually quite gentle and does not break the skin.

Some cats which bite get a reputation for bad temper, yet they are probably just feeling unwell. Cats are such stoic creatures that it is not always easy to spot when they are ill; the first sign may be when a usually friendly cat starts biting. Some cats may be unwell for a long time, perhaps with a painful cystitis or some other urological problem, before their condition deteriorates enough for their owners to notice that something is wrong. Veterinary treatment to cure the cat's ailment can also restore the cat's sunny temperament and make biting problems a thing of the past.

blaze

A contrasting marking, usually white, run-ning from the forehead to the nose. For ex-ample, Mitted Ragdolls may have white blazes on their noses.

bleeding (external)

Press on the bleeding area using a clean cloth or bandage to stop the flow. If bleeding con-tinues, press on the pressure points: for the head and neck an artery runs in a groove in the lower part of the shoulder where it meets the neck; for a forelimb injury press on the artery where it crosses the bone 2–5cm (¾–2in) above the inside of the elbow joint; on the hind limbs press where the artery crosses the bone on the inner thigh, and for tail injuries press on the artery on the underside of the tail.

If a tail or leg is severely injured, a tourni-quet can be applied but should be loosened every five minutes, if it takes longer than this to seek veterinary attention.

To apply a tourniquet: loop a bandage or scarf twice around the injured tail or leg above the wound and tie a half knot. Place a short stick on top of the half knot and complete tying the knot. Twist the stick until bleeding stops. Loosen every five minutes.

If there is a puncture wound in the chest and a sucking noise is heard, wind bandage around the body tightly enough to keep air from escaping and get your cat to a vet fast. If your cat has been shot with a gun or an arrow (sadly a not-uncommon occurrence), don't attempt to remove whatever caused the injury but press a sterile pad around the site, bandage, and take your cat to a vet.

If your cat's ear is bleeding – a common wound among fighting toms – hold a pad on the ear, covering both sides. Ears will bleed copiously, but should stop within five minutes. If not, take your cat to a vet.

See also **bandaging**. With all bleeding, watch out for signs of **shock** – especially if the bleeding is copious – and treat accordingly.

bleeding (internal)

Signs of internal bleeding are pale gums, rapid pulse, rapid breathing, bleeding from ears, nose or mouth.

Internal bleeding may be caused by an accident. Or if a cat has eaten a mouse or rat which has eaten poison it may suffer from internal bleeding as vermin poisons, such as Warfarin, stop blood clotting. You may notice blood spots on the gums.

Keep your cat warm and comfortable until it is possible to transport it to a vet. Handle it very gently or you will make the bleeding worse.

blood in urine

This can be a symptom of a serious urological problem and veterinary attention should be sought without delay.

blue

Blue is the correct term for the colour most of us would call grey. The colour is an optical illusion caused by **dilution**, which scatters and reflects black pigmentation so that we see it as blue.

Bobtail

See **Japanese Bobtail**.

body language

It is not difficult to tell exactly how your cat is feeling – all you have to do is observe its body language. A happy cat will walk tall – its ears and head will be carried high and its tail will stick straight up into the air. The cat will almost be on tiptoes if welcoming you and may bounce into the air to make itself even taller. It will rub its face and chin against you and try to reach your face if possible. This is because a cat's scent glands are on chin, lips and anus and it is marking you with its scent to show other cats who you belong to. There are scent glands on the paws too and cats stropping on furniture transfer their scent to it, marking it as their own.

Tails are eloquent. Straight up means happy, curved over at the tip means very happy, carried low shows a cautious cat, drooping sideways displays a lack of interest. A wildly-thrashing tail shows anger, while a tail being slowly whipped from side to side shows an alert cat who might decide to become angry.

Ears held upright mean that a cat is alert and happy, while slightly-swivelled ears show extreme happiness. Flattened ears are an indication of a fighting or defensive mood, as a cat will flatten its ears in a fight to protect them from damage.

Half-closed eyes show contentment and slow and deliberate blinking is used to signal that a cat has no evil intentions towards another cat. If you blink at your cat and it blinks back, it is considered by some to be the

*The Bombay, traditionally said to resemble
the black panther (page 26)*

equivalent of a kiss! But don't stare at your cat
– this is considered threatening behaviour.
Cats will stare fixedly at one another before
engaging in a fight. Often, if you wish to
prevent a fight, all you have to do is place
something in the cats' line of sight. If they
cannot see one another, they won't bother to
fight.

This is also the reason why cats always go to
people who dislike them. If someone who
likes cats enters a room, they will stare at the
cat, which will unnerve it. Someone who

dislikes cats won't look at it, so the cat will feel
secure and seek out the ailourophobe. It is a
waste of time telling these people that all they
have to do to be left alone is stare hard at the
cat – secretly they are quite pleased to have
been singled out for attention.

Whiskers will also move into different positions in response to mood. When fighting, the
whiskers will be drawn back and will empha-
sise the snarl. Pleasurable anticipation will
draw them forward.

Yawning is a sign of reassurance, so, if you

would like a nervous cat to settle down, yawn frequently but don't look at it! An anxious cat will twitch its ears and lick its lips rapidly. A very nervous cat will show the **flehmen response** – gasping and inhaling air through its slightly-open mouth. It is literally tasting and smelling the air for danger with a unique organ which allows it to do this – the **Jacobson's organ**.

Bombay (see page 25)

The Bombay breed received its name from the early breeders who thought these shiny black cats looked like Indian black panthers. The first Bombays appeared in the USA as a result of a cross between a brown **Burmese** and a black **American Shorthair**. They are now beginning to enjoy popularity in Europe.

Their short, satin-like coat is their most outstanding feature. It is more intensely black than that of other black cats, with a unique shine, said to be like black patent leather. The short coat means they are very easy to groom.

Bombays are active extroverts, loving to climb and play. They are friendly, sweet-tempered and affectionate, revelling in attention and enjoying any fuss made of them. They have very active purrs and are otherwise quiet voiced.

boredom

According to popular belief, cats don't suffer from boredom. The truth is that cats, being highly-intelligent creatures, suffer dreadfully from boredom. Yes, they will sleep a large part of the day but, when they wake, they enjoy – and must have – company, entertainment and play. Cats left alone all day will become maladjusted and may become destructive. Prospective owners have asked me which cats have placid and 'undestructive' temperaments because they are at work all

day. They have had the experience of owning several pedigree kittens at different times, which had, after a few months, started ripping up wallpaper and carpets. They did not realise that any kitten would become destructive under these circumstances, and that their current lifestyle is unsuited to owning a cat. If your lifestyle is similar, don't put a cat through the misery of hours of daily boredom.

breeding (as a source of income)

The above heading will produce loud laughter from any breeder who sees it. Most breeders do not expect to make money from their cats – which is just as well because they don't. They look on cat breeding as an interesting and enjoyable hobby, during the course of which they hope to help improve their chosen breed. So if you want to get into cat breeding for the money, think again.

Where living creatures are concerned, profit and loss accounts are meaningless. An infection could wipe out your entire 'stock' overnight. Even if your venture into breeding goes relatively smoothly, you will have to buy a kitten and wait for at least a year until she is old enough to breed. During that time and, of course, during her pregnancy and lactation, she must be receiving the very best quality food. She will also need various items of equipment to keep her happy (such as a scratching post, a climbing frame, etc) and some equipment to keep her or her kittens safe (for example, a pen to keep the kittens secure when you are not supervising them).

A stud cat is required; if you buy a male kitten and wait for him to mature (another year at least) you must provide him with warm, well-built and secure stud quarters out of doors, or else put up with him spraying all over the house. Well-made stud houses and runs, on concrete bases, are not cheap. If you do not have your own stud cat, you will have to pay a stud fee to use another stud and you will need transport to take your cat there and bring her back again. You will also have to take her to a vet for a test for **Feline Leukaemia Virus** before the stud owner will accept her.

She may need veterinary treatment during her pregnancy or veterinary help with kittening, the kittens may pick up an infection or have some other problem and, before going to their new homes, they must be inoculated. Their mother feeds them for a month; after that you must provide top-quality food for two months. You must pay for advertising in order to sell the kittens and you will find selling them easier if you show your cats and build up your reputation in the pedigree cat world – an expensive and time-consuming business. If you want to go on holiday during the time your cat is in kitten or while the kittens are still with their mother, you cannot place them in a cattery. So you will need someone to kittensit, full-time, while you are away.

All this applies to pedigree kittens which have market value; so you can see it is not worth considering breeding non-pedigree kittens, which cannot even be given away at certain times of the year, such as the summer, because there are so many.

breeding quality

Breeding quality kittens are those which conform quite closely to the standard of points for that breed and are considered of good enough quality to breed from. A breeding quality kitten may cost slightly less than a **show quality** kitten, or, if it is a particularly good specimen, it may be sold for breeding *and* show. If it becomes a **Champion** or **Grand Champion**, its offspring will be worth correspondingly more.

breeding true

Before a breed of cat is accepted as a pedigree breed, it must be proved that it 'breeds true'. This means that it must pass on its physical characteristics to its offspring. For example, a tabby moggy will not breed true – her offspring may be longhaired or shorthaired, long-nosed or short-nosed, and of virtually any colour. An accepted pedigree cat is one of a breed which has bred true through at least three generations.

British Blue   (see page 53)

The British Blue is the blue variety of the **British Shorthair** and has copper or orange eyes. At the moment it appears to be the most sought-after of the British Shorthairs in the United Kingdom as one of their number is currently (1989) appearing on television in a cat food advertisement!

British Shorthair   (see page 145)

This is a compact, chunky breed, broader and with a rounder head than the **Foreign** Shorthair, but smaller than the **American Shorthair**. The British Shorthair could be said to be the original native British cat, and was very popular until the newer, longhaired breeds were first seen at shows at the end of the 19th century.

They are very intelligent, friendly cats, with a placid nature. They are gentle and lovable, showing great affection to their owners. For all that, they are very catty cats, and make good mousers. Sturdy and healthy, they have been bred in a wide range of colours, including white, black, blue, cream, tortoiseshell and tabby.

British Shorthairs are easy to groom; a quick daily application of a comb will help keep these lovely cats immaculate.

Brown Burmese with Blue Burmese kitten

brushing

See **grooming**.

Burmese   *(see above)*

Burmese cats are one of the few breeds which were imported into the United Kingdom from the USA rather than the other way round. They originated in Burma but, when they arrived in the USA, were ridiculed as being poor examples of the **Siamese** breed. They have long been recognised as a beautiful breed in their own right, full of character and personality.

They are active and can be very independent, especially as they get older, but do like attention. They are very friendly when they choose to be and are vocal, though not nearly so noisy as the Siamese. They can be trained to walk on a lead, a fortunate accomplishment because they are so adventurous and often figure in the 'lost and found' columns of local newspapers. Some Burmese breeders recommend that they be kept as **indoor cats**.

They are available in many colours, including brown, blue, cream, red, tortoiseshell, chocolate and lilac. Medium-sized, slender cats, they are usually heavier than they look. Grooming is simple with occasional brushing and some **hand grooming** to keep them looking their best.

There is a longhaired version of the Burmese, called the Tiffany. Cats of great beauty, they are said to be similar in personality to the Burmese but perhaps slightly shyer and less outgoing.

Burmilla and Burmoiré

These striking cats are the result of a love-match between a **Burmese** and a **Chinchilla**. The Burmilla's coat is short but fuller than that of the Burmese. In temperament they can be similar to the Burmese but a little shyer and quieter. They have charming personalities and are easy to care for. Their coats are silver with dark tipping and faint tabby markings.

The Burmoiré is similar in build and temperament with a coat that can be described as like watered silk. They are smoke cats; that is, their fur is dark on top with silver colouring underneath. Stroked 'with the grain' as you would normally stroke a cat, they appear black; stroke them in the opposite direction, however, and their fur turns to silver!

burns

Treat a burned paw as you would a burned finger. Immerse the affected area in cold water for at least five minutes. If your cat is struggling, wrap a towel round it to restrain it, leaving only the head and burned paw free. For larger burns, immerse your cat up to the neck in cold water for five minutes. If possible, ask someone to telephone the vet while you are doing this as the burn will require veterinary attention. The vet will then be alerted to your imminent arrival. Your cat can be wrapped in a wet towel during the journey to the veterinary surgery.

Do not apply any salves or ointments as they will have to be scraped off before the cat can be treated.

buying a cat or kitten

Think carefully and long before acquiring a(nother) cat or kitten. Ask yourself the following questions:

▷ *Can I afford one?* Not the cost of the cat itself, which is usually small, or nothing at all, but the cost of keep over the next 14 to 15 years. This is the lifespan of the average cat and it will cost you around £5,000 at today's prices over that period for food, litter, cattery and veterinary fees, inoculations and equipment. If there's a week when you are particularly short of cash, you can be sure that will be the week when your cat will fall ill, yet you owe your companion immediate veterinary attention when necessary. Could you cope?

▷ *Can I provide a suitable home?* You may have a lovely home but do you have a landlord who bans pets? He is not going to change his mind just because Tiddles is so cute. Tiddles will be evicted before he even moves in. Is the home stable and permanent? If you're hoping to live abroad next year, don't buy a cat. Quarantine and other regulations mean that few cats are taken abroad or brought back with their owners. And many cats bought because someone is moving in with a boyfriend or girlfriend find themselves in rescue shelters a few months later when the partnership splits up.

▷ *Can I accept the commitment?* Many cats are purchased 'because a cat is easier to look after than a dog'. A cat may not need to be taken for walks but it is not an 'easy' pet – perhaps no living creature could be described as 'easy'. A cat requires time and attention, companionship and caring. If you're at work all day and have a hectic social life, don't buy a cat. Can you imagine your cat still living with you in

15 or 20 years' time? If not, don't buy a cat.

▷ *Thinking of buying a cat for someone else?* In a word – don't. It's impossible to choose a living creature for another person but it's amazing how many phone calls cat breeders receive every Christmas asking to buy a kitten (or two) as a surprise pet. Some surprise! How anyone can possibly commit another human being to 15 years of caring for a living creature without the most thorough discussion first, I don't know. Reputable breeders, faced with this sort of query, refuse to sell their kittens through a third party. Christmas is also the wrong time to bring a new pet into the home because of the noise, disruption and chaos of the festive season. Rescue shelters and the best breeders and pet shops will refuse to sell cats at Christmas.

Where should you buy a cat once you have decided you can give it a good home?

▷ *Rescue shelters* are an excellent source of cats and kittens of all types. These shelters are over full from May throughout the summer but don't expect to take home a pet the day you choose it. Most shelters will arrange a home visit by one of their volunteers before parting with a cat. This is to discourage impulse buys and ensure that a genuine home is being offered. On at least one occasion, the home visit has turned up the information that the cat was wanted as 'bait' in cat-coursing. Needless to say, not only was the offer refused, but the prospective purchaser was placed on a blacklist, circulated to all shelters in the area. So don't be offended if the shelter checks you out – it is to protect the cats.

The cats and kittens in these shelters are not usually free. The shelters are charities and the cost of caring for the animals must be recouped. In some cases, a purchase price is quoted and in others, a donation is suggested. You can, however, make a financial saving by buying a cat from a shelter. If the cat is old enough, it will have been neutered and received its first inoculations. Shelter volunteers are usually only too pleased to advise new owners on the care of their pets.

▷ *Pet stores* are not recommended for the purchase of kittens, and fewer and fewer pet stores are now selling them. The reason is that cats and kittens are susceptible to many diseases which are easily passed from one to another if they are kept in close proximity. Only kittens from the same litter should be kept together; kittens from any other litter should be kept quite separate, for if one kitten has an ailment, it will rapidly spread to them all.

You should also see a kitten's mother before purchasing it to check on her general state of health; you will be unable to do this in a pet store. The kittens may also be too young to have left their mother; eight weeks is a reasonable age for non-pedigree kittens but the absolute minimum would be six weeks for exceptionally well-developed and healthy kittens.

▷ *Friends' cats* have kittens every summer because the friends haven't got round to having the cat spayed. This is how most people acquire their kittens. You will be able to see the mother cat and learn her history. You can arrange to take the kitten away at a suitable age and you will know if it has been wormed or inoculated.

▷ *Breeders* You should only come across breeders if you decide to purchase a pedigree kitten. There are hundreds of thousands of homeless non-pedigree kittens, so no-one should be deliberately breeding non-pedigree kittens for sale. (If you come across one, don't buy a kitten from them; too often their queens are nothing more than kitten factories.)

If you decide to buy a pedigree kitten, take your time about your choice. Decide on the breed you would like then visit a cat show if you can. Talk to the breeders of your chosen breed until you find one you like who has a good reputation – other breeders will soon tell you about the ones who *don't* have good reputations! Then, having found a good breeder, wait as long as you need to for a kitten and pay whatever is asked. A good breeder will ask a fair price. You may find another kitten of the same breed elsewhere at a lower price but it may not be such a high quality kitten and trying to save money in this way is always a false economy. See also **choosing a cat or kitten**.

C

CA

See **Cat Association of Britain**.

Caesarian delivery

Despite the cat's reputation for giving birth with ease, in some cases – for example, if a cat's pelvis is narrow – a Caesarian operation will be required. Named after Julius Caesar, who was reputed to have been born this way, a Caesarian does not affect a cat's ability to have subsequent litters.

Calico

The name in the USA for a **patched** tortoiseshell and white cat.

California Spangled Cat

See **Oriental Tabby** and **Spotted**.

calling

See **season**.

Cameo

Cameo is a colour of **Persian** where the undercoat is white and the hairtips are red, blue-cream or tortoiseshell. Many lines used crossings with **Chinchillas** to develop the Cameo in the 1950s when the first Cameos were bred. Pewters are members of the Cameo group of **Persians** and have a white undercoat tipped with black, giving the look of pewter. They have black-rimmed copper eyes.

Canadian Hairless   *(see opposite)*

See **Sphynx**.

cancer

Cancer is a word which strikes fear into the heart of any owner but it need not do so. Cancer in the cat can be treated in the same way as cancer in humans – using either radiation to destroy malignant cells or chemotherapy with drugs and chemicals to treat the condition. However, most feline cancers are treated surgically where possible.

Not every tumour is malignant; benign tumours will not threaten your cat's life. Be on the lookout for lumps or growths, especially if they are of irregular shape and grow quickly.

Early treatment is essential. If a malignant tumour is found and removed quickly, the cat could make a full and rapid recovery.

canker

A word sometimes used to cover a variety of ear problems. A cat will be seen to scratch its ears and shake its head. Don't try to treat the problem yourself – consult your vet. See also **ears**.

cannibalism

Kittens are extremely vulnerable for the first few weeks of their lives. If their mother is

*Sphynx kittens, the breed was originally called
the Canadian Hairless*

disturbed unnecessarily and becomes concerned for the safety of her offspring, she may be driven to kill them. Cats should have a cosy, quiet 'nest' in which to have their kittens and visitors should be barred for, if possible, the first month. A cat which kills her kittens will usually eat them. By doing so, she is absorbing high-quality protein which will make her stronger and enable her to have another litter of kittens sooner. If she feels they are in danger and may be killed anyway, killing them herself ensures their end is swift. A mother cat may also kill and eat a kitten if it is ill. By doing so, she will minimise the risk of any infection spreading to her other kittens.

Very young kittens may be killed by an entire tomcat which gains access to them. By killing the kittens, the tom ensures that the female will come into season more quickly, giving him a chance to mate with her and so perpetuate *his* genes. Hard luck on the genes of the father of the dead litter! Nature can seem brutal. Anyone whose cat has recently had kittens should ensure that, for the first few weeks of their lives, windows are kept closed, and doors and cat-flaps are locked at all times.

caramel

Name used in the USA for the fur colour chocolate; also called chestnut.

carrying baskets

A good carrying basket should last a cat's lifetime, so choose carefully. It will be needed every time you take your cat to a vet, to a holiday cattery, when you move house, and to shows, if you exhibit your cat.

My own preference is for plastic-coated wire carriers. These are rectangular in shape, with a carrying handle and a fastening latch which slots into a loop. They are extremely hygienic, being completely washable, and very strong. If you visit a cat show, these carriers are usually on sale at a discount price.

More picturesque are the wickerwork baskets with plastic-coated wire fronts. Although these give a cat more privacy, you will find they ladder your tights or snag your trousers. They are also almost impossible to wash or disinfect, so, if you have more than one cat, consider another type of carrier.

Some carriers combine a mesh front with a plastic or glass fibre body. These give a cat privacy and are easy to wash and disinfect. However, they are not as strong as the all-wire carrier, so will not last as long. (One person of my acquaintance was travelling to a London cat show on the Underground when the door closed on her carrier, squashing it and allowing her cat to escape. The cat ran down the tunnel, hotly pursued by the driver, who fortunately managed to catch it.)

A new version of the plastic carrier has wheels and a towing handle. This is a boon to people with overweight cats, which is most of us. (If you feel that's an exaggeration think of a leopard or a cheetah!) The carrier is available in truly enormous sizes.

When choosing a carrier, buy one slightly bigger than you think you will need. The bigger the carrier, the higher the price, but a too-small carrier is worse than useless.

If your cat is reluctant to emerge from its carrier when required, you will find it easier to remove it if the carrier has a top, rather than a side, opening.

Don't let your cat equate the appearance of its carrier with a visit to the vet. Take the carrier out of its storage-place every so often, open it and allow your cat to play in and out of it. By doing so, the carrier will become familiar and not an object of dread.

If your cat is nervous about travelling,

sprinkle a little catnip in the bottom of the carrier to make its journey more pleasant.

Cat Association of Britain (CA)

Registration organisation set up in 1983 in competition with the longer-established GCCF. It fulfils many of the same registration, licensing and welfare roles and also recognises a number of breeds of cats which the GCCF does not yet recognise. Cat Association shows are generally regarded as more interesting than GCCF shows as the cats are judged on the American ring judging system, ie the cats are brought to the judge who describes, aloud, its good and bad points to his/her audience. Pens at CA shows may be decorated. See also **showing**.

cat clubs

Cat clubs are of two types: breed clubs and geographical clubs. Breed clubs bring together groups of people interested in a particular breed of cat, for example, Siamese, Chinchillas, Korats. Geographical clubs cover a specific area of the country and any enthusiasts in that area can join the club. Most cat club members are breeders of pedigree cats, or owners of pedigree cats; although membership is open to everyone, not many non-pedigree cat owners join cat clubs.

Clubs usually require a prospective member to be proposed and seconded by existing members of the club; membership is not usually turned down unless the applicant is known to mistreat her/his cats or to be in some way undesirable. Each club is affiliated, or hopes to become affiliated, to one of the registration organisations.

As well as having a social function, the clubs help members to increase their knowledge of cats through talking to other, more experienced members, or through any lectures or teach-ins the clubs may organise. Each club has its own newsletter and this will keep members up to date with what is happening with 'their' breed or in their area. Each club will also keep lists of members who are cat breeders so anyone wanting to buy a pedigree kitten (whether a club member or not) should contact the relevant breed club to ask for a recommended breeder.

cat flaps

Cat flaps, or cat doors, are extremely useful for many owners but their use has possibly made owners a little lazy. Flaps save time and effort for an owner who no longer has to open and close doors or windows for their cat, but they have the disadvantage that the owner no longer knows whether their cat is indoors or out. If a cat flap is fitted, it must be of the locking type, so that an owner can call the cat indoors at night and lock the flap behind it. There are other times when it is vital that the flap is kept locked and that no other cats have access to your home: when there are young kittens, when a cat is ill, and when you want to ensure no cat can come into your home and steal food – or spray.

Flaps range from the basic plastic model which will swing and rattle in the breeze to de luxe models operated by selective electronic keys worn on a cat's collar.

When buying a cat flap, check that:

▷ the amount of pressure required to open the flap is low. Some need 3 ounces of effort to open – others require 12 to 18 ounces.

▷ your cat cannot trap its paw in the flap. If you push your finger through the flap and withdraw it – and it gets caught – your cat could trap its paw in the same way. If you are not at home,

your cat could be trapped for hours.
▷ do you want your cat to wear a collar?
It will have to in order to open some
types of flap. Is your cat an escape
artist? If so, it will cost you extra to
keep replacing the collar and key.

Remember that electro-magnetic flaps
mean that a cat has to wear a magnetic key on
its collar which will attract loose metal, wires,
nails, etc. Electronic cat doors are operated
by a key on a cat's collar which transmits a
signal – how swiftly do these doors close
behind your cat? If not instantaneous, neighbouring cats will take advantage and jump in
too.

Remember also that cats like to see where
they are going – see-through flaps may be
more appreciated. Side-opening flaps may be
less likely to trap paws. Flaps should incorporate some form of draught-excluder otherwise they will not only be noisy but will let in
draughts. And all cat-flaps should be installed
at more than arm's length from a door lock –
otherwise burglars can reach in and open your
door.

In my opinion it's easier to open and close
doors!

cat 'flu

See **Feline Respiratory Disease**.

catnip (catmint)

Catnip, also called catmint, is a herb belonging to the mint family which has been used by
man since the days of Ancient Egypt and by
cats for even longer. It has a remarkable effect
on cats, in that it stimulates and relaxes them
at the same time. Sprinkle a pinch of catnip on
the floor and a stressed cat will relax, purring,
rolling on the herb, sniffing it and eating it.
Rub it on a scratching post to persuade your

cat to use it, sprinkle it in your cat's basket to
make a trip to the vet a little more pleasant,
perk up appetite by occasionally sprinkling a
little on food and stuff toys with it. You can
even make it into tea and drink it yourself as
an aid to digestion.

The chemical which gives cats their buzz is
nepetalactone which is activated by smell and
works on a cat's nervous system. It is non-
addictive and completely safe, as long as you
keep your cat indoors for half an hour after
using catnip, to allow the effects to wear off –
otherwise your happy cat might blunder
straight into an unfriendly dog. And some
breeders believe that it can cause miscarriage
in a pregnant queen; so you may choose to
limit its use.

Catnip can be purchased in its dried form
from herbalists and health food stores. It
should be stored in an airtight container (an
empty coffee jar is ideal) as, like any herb, it
will lose its essential oils if left exposed to the
air. Catnip toys should also be stored in airtight containers and brought out for twenty
minutes' play at a time.

You can also grow your own catnip from
seed in pots on your windowsill. If you love all
the neighbourhood cats as well as your own,
you can grow it out of doors from May to June.
You will be extremely popular with the local
felines, and bees, which also enjoy the plants.

The type you should grow is *Nepeta cata-
ria*, not the ornamental varieties, which will
have no effect on your cat. A sunny position is
best, although the soil need not be rich, the
root system takes some time to become established. When transplanting, try not to crush
the stems or leaves, otherwise the scent will
attract cats which will eat the plants. Plants
can be protected with 'crowns' of wire mesh
or by placing lampshades, without the fabric,
over them.

*Young male Chartreuse (page 39); compare
with the British Blue (page 53)*

Cut the catnip's stems when they are about 45cm tall, as this is when they contain the most concentrated amount of oil in the leaves. Catnip is dried the same way as any other herb, by bunching and hanging up in a cool, dark place until brittle, or by placing in a very slow oven. Store in an airtight container until needed.

It is said that only about eight out of ten cats are susceptible to catnip, but I've never met one that wasn't.

cat scratch fever

Few people have heard about cat scratch disease or link a mild fever, headache, an outbreak of spots on hand or arm, and perhaps a swelling in the armpit with a scratch from their cat sustained several weeks before. The disease is believed to be caused by bacterial infection which enters at the site of a scratch from a cat which may have no symptoms itself. As it is impossible to know if a cat is a carrier, cat scratch disease is yet another reason for careful hygiene. If scratched or bitten by a cat, always flush out the wound thoroughly with running water then treat with antiseptic.

catteries

If you are lucky enough to go away for a summer holiday, when do you book it? January. If you are booking a summer holiday, when should you book your cat's accommodation? January! The best cattery accommodation becomes fully booked soon after Christmas.

Expect to spend as much time choosing your cat's holiday accommodation as you spent choosing your own. (At least after you have chosen your cat's accommodation you can use it year after year – unlike your own holiday arrangements.) Don't just pick a cattery out of the telephone book; ask around your friends and family who may be able to personally recommend a cattery. But do not rely on personal recommendation; telephone for an appointment to view possible catteries. Ask to see all over the premises; some unscrupulous cattery owners have beautiful accommodation in full view and unhygienic prisons hidden at the back, where most of the boarders stay. It does happen. Owners have booked their cats into a cattery, and have seen them being accommodated in modern runs, only to collect them several weeks later, dirty, ill and thin, from little hutches hidden at the back. If the owner won't show you all over the premises, don't book.

The ideal cattery should keep cats well separated, with their own houses in individual runs with solid floors which can easily be disinfected. The run areas should *never* be communal; accommodation should *never* be shared, except by cats from the same household. There should be a metre between each run or an impermeable 'sneeze barrier' so that, if an infected cat sneezes, it does not do so over your cat, passing on infection.

For the same reason *never* book your cat into a cattery which has numbers of pens piled on top of one another. There is a very high risk of infection at this type of cattery. I know of at least one cattery of this type run by someone with the very best of intentions, but the first time a cat incubating an illness is taken into that cattery, the disease will spread through every cat staying there. Avoid such places, literally, like the plague.

The cattery should have a double door system before any cat is reached. Each unit should have a door, leading to a corridor off which lead doors to the cats' runs. Catteries which do not have this safety device have been known to lose cats.

The houses should have individual, safe heating, in case of cold weather. Your cat should have plenty of space to roam around and a comfortable, high place to sleep. Try to find a cattery which does not board dogs; they upset many cats. If the cattery is a kennels too, ensure the dogs are well out of sight and smell of the cats.

There should be no bad smells when you look around a cattery. Feeding bowls should be clean and water bowls should be filled and clean. Litter trays, ditto. Cats already staying there should look content. All accommodation should be sterilised between boarders. Staff should show interest in your cat's special requirements. However, if you request a special diet for your cat, this may cost extra, even if you supply the food yourself, because of the extra trouble of treating your cat as an individual! A cat should be allowed its own, familiar-smelling blanket and a few favourite toys.

All reputable catteries will insist that your cat's inoculations are up to date before they will accept it for boarding. Don't use a cattery that does not insist on this. If other cats in the cattery are not inoculated, they could be harbouring all sorts of illnesses which they will transmit to other cats – maybe yours.

challenge certificates

A winner of a pedigree breed class at a show may be awarded a challenge certificate if it is of a high enough standard. Challenge certificates (CCs) may be withheld from a winning cat if, in the opinion of the judge, it does not reach the required standard. If a cat collects three challenge certificates from three different judges at three shows (GCCF) it becomes a champion. Under CA rules, it is possible for a cat to collect three challenge certificates at one show.

Champion

A Champion is a cat which is awarded three **challenge certificates**. In the USA, a cat becomes a Champion when it has won six winner's ribbons under four different judges.

Championship Show

A Championship Show is one where **challenge certificates** can be awarded. Cat clubs can each hold one Championship Show a year.

changing diet

You may have to change your cat's diet several times during its life, either on veterinary recommendation or because your pocket is feeling the pinch. Always do so gradually. If you try to change your cat's diet too rapidly, it may refuse the new food or, if it accepts it, it will suffer diarrhoea. So mix a little of the new food into a lot of the old food until that has been accepted. Then increase quantities of the new, decreasing quantities of the old, until your cat has a bowl full of new food.

Chartreuse, Chartreux, Karthusian (see page 37)

Strangely, for a French cat, the Chartreuse is not recognised as a separate breed in France. It competes alongside **British Blues**, as it does in the United Kingdom. However, in the USA it has breed status and competes in its own breed class.

The Chartreuse is reputed to have been developed in the Middle Ages by Carthusian monks, who also produce the potent liqueur, Chartreuse. Some 400 years ago these cats were used to provide both fur and meat! Their survival undoubtedly rests with their other talent – that of rat-catcher *extraordinaire*.

The Chartreuse is an extremely powerful,

muscular cat, famed and bred for its hunting prowess. Its coat is perhaps its most unusual feature, being thick and woolly. According to the standard of points, the coat should break like a sheep's fleece at neck and flanks.

In France, the Chartreuse is known as the dog-like cat. They are a delightful combination of the active breeds and the placid breeds. Gentle and quiet, they chirrup rather than miaow. Aficionados of the breed describe them as looking, and behaving, like their original breeders – jolly fat friars with an extraordinary sense of humour!

cheese

Cheese is an excellent source of protein, minerals and vitamins (except vitamin C). As such, a little cheese can be a valuable addition to your cat's diet and most cats adore it. Go easy on the quantity, however, as too much can make your cat sick if it is not used to it. Cottage cheese is sometimes given to young kittens as part of one of their daily meals.

chestnut

Name used in the USA for the fur colour chocolate; also called caramel.

Chinchilla   (see opposite)

The origins of the Chinchilla are something of a mystery but this cat, which now has sparkling white fur, seems to have been bred from cats with coloured coats. The earlier Chinchillas were darker than they are today, although they are now also being bred in colours, such as gold. However, most Chinchillas are white, lightly ticked with black, with black-rimmed, green eyes. They are not as **cobby** as other longhairs, as they are usually smaller and finer-boned.

Their beautiful coat is fine and dense and owners should be prepared to devote some time to grooming. Although they are considered to be no more demanding care-wise than other longhairs, an owner must be prepared to spend time in daily brushing and combing to keep the coat in first-class condition. Moulting could be a problem for the houseproud owner.

Chinchillas are quiet voiced and extremely intelligent, being sensitive and aware of all that is going on. Some, because of this sensitivity, do not like too much handling, and a few can be downright grumpy. Although they are active, with plenty of energy, they do not need as much space as many other breeds and will settle happily to life in a flat. They have a reputation for hardiness.

The name, Chinchilla, was agreed on by early breeders but the cat's fur has no similarity to that of the rodent of the same name which is bred for its fur and is now a popular pet.

chocolate

A brown fur colour, lighter than **seal**, and usually a warm shade.

choosing a cat or kitten

Having decided what sort of cat or kitten you will buy and where you will buy it from (see **buying a cat or kitten**), you then have to find a healthy one.

If buying a kitten, try to buy one from a home which looks clean and where the owners seem to know what they are doing. Always ask to see the kitten's mother and try to gauge her state of health. If she is ill or run-down, her kitten will be too, although it may not yet be apparent. Even if the kitten is 'free', don't take it. By the time you have paid the resulting veterinary fees, this free kitten will be expensive indeed.

Don't always choose the kitten which

The Chinchilla's pure white coat is actually tipped with black

comes rushing to greet you. It is probably the show-off of the litter – and who wants to live with a show-off? But, equally, don't choose the one which holds back either, unless you have a totally unassuming personality, which this kitten will match (unless it is ill – another reason why it may be holding back). For most people, the 'average' kitten in the litter will be the right one, the normally curious, active kitten which will come to inspect you when it feels like it.

Pick the kitten up and scrutinise it closely, whether it is free or costs a fortune. Its fur should be clean with no mats or tangles, especially around the anal area. Lift the tail and check there are no signs of diarrhoea. Part the fur; if you see small black specks (easy to see on a pale-coloured kitten but difficult on a black one) these may be flea faeces. Check for these around ears, under the chin and by the mouth and at the top of the tail.

Kittens should feel solid, not skin and bone, and should be well-fleshed. They should not have a pot belly, which may be a sign of worms.

Look in ears and mouth. Teeth should be white and gums a healthy pink; not pale and not red. Ears should look clean inside and have no smell. If the kitten is shaking its head or scratching its ears, there may be an infection present.

Eyes should be bright and clean with no signs of a visible **third eyelid**.

The kitten should be, at the very least, six weeks old before it leaves its mother – eight weeks is better. If it is a pedigree kitten, it should be twelve weeks old as pedigree kittens mature more slowly. Whatever age the kitten is, it should be weaned – eating solid food – before it leaves its mother.

The same checks apply to an adult cat, if you are giving one a home.

But, adult or kitten, never buy it because you feel sorry for it. If it is not being kept properly, or receiving essential veterinary attention, report the matter to your local animal cruelty organisation. Don't take it home with you, especially if you already have a cat, as any illness the newcomer has will almost certainly be passed on to your other cat(s).

Even if the newcomer appears to be in the best of health, if you already own a cat, quarantine your new pet for at least a week to ensure that no illness is developing unsuspected (see **quarantine**).

classic

A tabby pattern also known as marbled or blotched. There is a black 'butterfly' across the shoulders and whorls along the sides.

claws

Claws are a very important part of a cat's armoury. Not only are they effective weapons, but they are strategically important, allowing a cat to avoid confrontation by climbing quickly out of danger. Cats will keep their claws in good shape by themselves. Walking on hard surfaces will blunt them, but stropping them on trees or scratching posts will sharpen them again.

Owners may not be thrilled by their cat's sharp claws digging into their laps, in which case a little regular trimming is permissible. Hold your cat firmly, place your thumb on top of the paw and your finger on the pawpad. Press gently and the claws will unsheath. Take off just the tip of the claw using nail scissors, nail clippers, or claw trimmers. Be very careful not to take off more than the tip. *Never* cut down to the quick which will bleed copiously. The quick is pinkish-coloured and can be seen if you look carefully at the claws.

Keep well away from it when cutting. See also **declawing**.

cleft palate

Occasionally, a kitten is born with a cleft palate when the bones across the roof of the mouth fail to join together leaving an opening between the mouth and the nasal passages. Sometimes milk can be seen bubbling from the kitten's nose. This is a genetic defect and varying degrees of deformity occur, in some cases it is so severe that the kitten cannot suck. In such cases euthanasia is the only answer. In less serious cases, hand rearing may prove successful but the kitten should be neutered at the correct time so that the defect cannot be passed on.

climbers, climbing frames

Nowadays there is a remarkable amount of indoor furniture being made for cats. As well as four-poster beds, carpet-covered bungalows and play tubes, there is a wide range of cat climbers. These are enjoyed by every cat but particularly by indoor cats, as they are an indoor substitute for trees.

Climbers come in different shapes and sizes but most are carpet-covered or partially carpet-covered in colours to match the décor of your room. Some reach from floor to ceiling while others are free-standing. All consist of an upright, which may be covered by carpet or rope, and shelves for cats to rest on. Some also incorporate a box at the bottom with several holes for access.

Cat climbers provide cats with a great deal of fun, especially if they have a feline friend they can chase. They provide excellent exercise and cats enjoy sleeping high up, on the shelves. The uprights will also be used by cats to strop.

club class

At a cat show, a club class is one held by a particular cat club and only members of that club may enter their cats.

cobby

A description of a body-type. A cat so described is a chunky cat, with short legs and a body in proportion. The best-known example of a cobby body-type is the **Persian**.

collars

There are two cat-collaring factions in this world: those who are very strongly for and those who are very strongly against.

The 'for' faction say, quite rightly, that the owners of a lost cat or a cat which has met with an accident may never know what has happened to their pet if they cannot be traced by identification on the collar.

The 'against' faction say, also quite rightly, that cats wearing collars can be choked or strangled by them if they become caught on branches or nails. The fact that collars are sold with 'safety' elastic in them cuts no ice with the 'against' faction as often the elastic does not have enough 'give' in it to allow a cat to escape entanglement.

So what do you do? If you feel you must put a collar on your cat, ensure it fits correctly. That is, you should be able to insert a finger between the collar and your cat's neck. More than one finger and the collar is too loose; your cat may entangle its chin or paws in it. Do buy collars with 'safety' elastic in them and, as an additional safeguard, partially cut through the elastic. Then, if your cat becomes entangled, the elastic should snap.

Don't bother belling your cat in an attempt to prevent it catching **birds** – it doesn't work.

Colourpoint (see opposite)

This breed is called the Himalayan in the USA because the **Himalayan gene** gives the dark colouring to the points. Colourpoints, as they are known in the UK, are longhairs with the **Siamese** coat pattern and are classed as a colour variant of **Persian**.

Their temperament obviously owes a lot to their ancestry and they are a delightful mix of Siamese (total extrovert) and Persian (placid lapcat). They adore attention and will make sure they get it. Each one will have its own way of ensuring that its owner will give it time and attention. They are very affectionate, robust cats and love an outdoor life. As they like a degree of liberty, they would enjoy a large garden to play in.

Grooming, as with most longhairs, needs to be on a daily basis, especially during the spring moult.

Colourpoint kittens, like those of other breeds coloured by the Himalayan gene, are born without the dark colouring of the points. These darken with age. Points colours include chocolate, blue, red and tortoiseshell.

combing

See **grooming**.

condition

A cat in good condition will have sleek, shiny fur, bright eyes – although not necessarily a wet nose – and will look at peace with the world. An out-of-condition cat will have a rough, **staring coat**, dull eyes and will appear listless. Worming your cat or improving its diet may improve its condition. If in any doubt, as always, consult your vet. There are conditioners, nutritional supplements that act as a 'tonic', specifically formulated for cats, but if your cat is healthy and well-nourished these should not be necessary.

constipation

The majority of cat-owners (68% at the last count) may never know whether their cat is constipated or not, because they do not provide it with a litter tray. Therefore, they never see their cat crouched over it, straining to pass faeces. They may notice other signs: a miserable look, dullness, lack of interest. Constipation is a particular problem in the older cat, whose muscle tone will not be as good as it once was.

Products specifically formulated for cat constipation are available and should be given according to directions. Medicinal liquid paraffin may help shift any blockage. Give one teaspoonful daily for no more than three or four days. Liquid paraffin coats the walls of the stomach and intestines, inhibiting the absorption of vitamins, so a cat dosed with it regularly would suffer a vitamin deficiency.

As always, if in the slightest doubt, consult your vet. Some constipation problems are so severe that an operation is necessary. It is also important to differentiate between constipation and urinary problems, which can be potentially lethal if not treated quickly in the correct manner.

consumer goods

There is an amazing range of consumer goods available specifically for the cat. However, you may never come across most of them. Most pet stores are so short of space that they cannot possibly carry more than a tiny percentage of what is available for any pet. So, if you want to buy some cat products, where do you get them?

Pet stores can usually order what you want if you *know* what you want. However, you might not even know that the product which would make your life much easier exists.

Blue-Point Colourpoint Persian

If you can, visit a large cat show. These shows usually attract cat equipment suppliers who stock an incredible range of items. If you don't want to buy the product on the day, most will have a mail order facility. However, by buying at a show, you not only save postage but may be able to take advantage of a special show discount.

Alternatively you can buy one of the many cat magazines which are published and which carry mail order advertisements for cat products.

contraception

Many owners, concerned about putting their cats through the surgical procedure of neutering, wonder if other forms of contraception are a viable alternative. There are only two methods of contraception available for cats: surgical neutering which is permanent and, in the long run, probably safest too, or the contraceptive pill or injection. The pill has been available since the 1960s but is still not widely used and is treated with some suspicion by many breeders, despite its usefulness when they wish to delay the pregnancy of their breeding queens.

Tablets or injections are given at the first sign of calling and are only available from vets. Tablets are given for a number of days and the dose needs to be carefully calculated according to the weight of the cat. Injections can be longer-lasting, given once every few months. *Expert* veterinary advice should be taken before you decide whether or not to use contraception for your cat because, of course, it has both advantages and disadvantages.

The contraceptive pill (or injection) utilises a synthetic hormone to prevent a cat from coming into season with the result that, if she does not come into season, she cannot become pregnant.

convalescence

Cats are often said to display feminine qualities. However, in convalescence they display particularly masculine qualities – they feel exceedingly sorry for themselves and need to be jollied along constantly.

TLC (tender loving care) is so vitally important for the convalescent cat that without it some will give up the struggle and die. So a sick cat should be kept warm, quiet and secure. Running eyes or nose should be wiped clean regularly and the cat should be helped to its litter tray, if necessary. A supply of clean, fresh water should be left nearby. Tempting food should be supplied; food which smells strongly will attract an ailing cat. If your cat is unable to eat solid food, liquidise the food with a little water, stock or milk. Brush or comb your cat every day as it will be unable to groom itself. And be patient; once your cat turns the corner it will astound you with the speed of its recovery.

Cornish Rex

See **Rex**.

coughing

There are a number of causes of coughing:

▷ The most common cause is probably the presence of swallowed hair at the back of the throat. The cat coughs – sometimes constantly – to try to dislodge it. A piece of grass, fish bone or piece of dry food caught at the back of the throat will cause the same reaction. A teaspoon of liquid paraffin will probably help ease the irritant down the throat.

▷ A foreign body stuck in the throat which is big enough to obstruct breathing will make the cat drool and paw at its mouth. It will look very uncomfortable and will cough explosively. Veterinary attention should be sought immediately.

▷ **Worms** can cause coughing. Treat with an appropriate dewormer.

▷ **Allergies** can cause coughing. If a cat coughs mainly during the winter, it may be allergic to something indoors, perhaps fumes or dust from a heating system. Summer coughing may point to an outdoor allergy, for example, pollen.

▷ Growths in the mouth, infections, heart disease or tonsilitis may all cause coughing. Consult your vet.

cryptorchid

A male cat whose testicles have not descended, a definite fault in a show cat. See also **monorchid**.

Cypress or Cyprus

Name by which the tabby is sometimes known in the United Kingdom.

cyst

A sebaceous cyst is a fluid-filled lump found on the skin as a result of the sebaceous gland being blocked. Other types of cyst can occur throughout the body. Check with your vet if you find any lumps on your cat's body. These may be harmless cysts but it is possible they could be tumours which will require immediate attention.

cystitis

Cystitis means inflammation on the wall of the bladder and is an acutely uncomfortable condition, yet few owners realise that cats of both sexes can suffer from it and it is even quite common. It is most often caused by bacteria in the bladder which become a problem if the cat does not urinate frequently enough to get rid of them before they do any harm.

Some cases of cystitis are so mild that the owner does not notice anything is wrong; as the condition worsens the cat may begin to urinate on carpets and furniture and may be seen straining on its litter tray. It may also cry out in pain. Urgent veterinary attention is essential.

Antibiotics will probably be prescribed, along with urine acidifiers, but lifestyle changes are important to prevent a recurrence of the problem.

▷ Encourage your cat to drink more. If it doesn't drink much, start adding salt to its food – about an eighth of a teaspoonful daily. This will have no harmful effects on the cat but will make it thirsty. Obviously, ensure there is clean water for it to drink at all times. If your cat drinks milk with no ill effects, add water to the milk so that liquid intake is increased.

▷ Don't feed dry foods. These make urine more concentrated and you should be trying to make it much less concentrated. Feed moist foods and add water to them.

▷ If you have not already done so, supply a litter tray, and keep it clean at all times to encourage your cat to use it. If your cat prefers to urinate out of doors, provide a tray anyway but put your cat outside at least four times a day.

D

dam

Not a swear word but the mother of a cat –
seldom seen or used except on pedigree
forms.

damage

Usually, you will not be held responsible for
any damage caused by your cat, as cats are not
subject to the laws of trespass, if that damage
is due to normal feline behaviour. However,
anything other than normal behaviour could
involve you in liability. And the law of trespass is a two-edged sword. If your cat goes on
a neighbour's property and eats poisonous
slug pellets, you have no redress in law, not
even for the considerable veterinary expenses
which may be incurred.

dander

The top layer of skin (the epidermis) is constantly being rubbed off and replaced from
the layer beneath (the dermis). As the exposed epidermis ages, tiny flakes of skin drop
off into the fur, forming dander, which is
removed by brushing or by the cat's grooming.

deafness

If your cat does not turn its head to follow a
sound, swivelling its ears to locate the noise,
it may be deaf. Deafness can be caused by ear
infection, a reaction to some drugs or by a
build-up of wax, in which case it may be
temporary. Veterinary treatment should
alleviate the problem. If your cat is past
middle age, its hearing may become less
acute. Blue-eyed white cats are sometimes,
but not always, deaf, because the gene which
gives the white colour produces degenerative
changes in the cochlea, the spiral passage of
the inner ear. Odd-eyed cats may be deaf in
one ear – the ear on the side of the blue eye.

If you have a deaf, or partially-deaf, cat it
will need extra care. It might be kinder to
keep it as an **indoor cat** from kittenhood away
from the danger of traffic and predators.

declawing

Declawing is a surgical procedure to remove
cats' claws so that no damage is caused to their
owners' soft furnishings. Advocates of declawing believe that it is no more unkind than
neutering which, they say, is also altering a
cat to adapt it to living with humans. Nevertheless, veterinary associations in the United
Kingdom abhor the practice and it is unlikely
that any British vet would carry out the operation.

Declawing is painful for the cat and it is
possible for the claw to regrow, which neces-
sitates a further operation. As with any operation, there is always a risk of infection or
haemorrhage. Declawed cats are unable to
grip, climb, or properly defend themselves.

Devon Rex adult with Tabby Devon Rex kitten
(pages 50 and 125)

Some become emotionally disturbed, distrustful of their owners or vets, and may start biting.

Owners of cats which damage furniture can take steps to discourage this; see **scratching furniture** and **claws**.

dehydration

Dehydration – loss of water from the body tissues – can follow severe diarrhoea or vomiting. Ensure that clean drinking water is always available if your cat is ill. Food can be liquidised to increase fluid intake and can be spoon-fed if necessary. When severely dehydrated, a cat's skin becomes inelastic. If you gather a fold of skin on the back or neck of a dehydrated cat, the skin does not immediately slide back into place. This is called 'tenting', and means that immediate veterinary attention is essential.

dermatitis

Dermatitis is an inflammation of the skin. The most common cause of feline dermatitis is allergy to flea saliva. Some cats become so sensitive that just one bite can result in skin irritation. Small lumps can be felt on the cat's skin, often across the neck and around the chin and tail, also along the back. A cat with dermatitis will scratch and lick at the sores, usually making them worse. Other causes of dermatitis include too much fish in the diet, food allergy, vitamin deficiency or hormone imbalances. Causes are varied and so is the treatment; it will include altering any dietary or hormonal imbalances.

Devon Rex   (see page 48)

See **Rex**.

dewclaw

The dewclaw is found on the inside of the leg above the front paw. It is really a vestigial 'thumb' and serves no useful purpose. It is often removed on puppies, but never on cats or kittens, unless it becomes badly damaged, which is surprisingly rare.

diabetes

Many owners are surprised to learn that cats can suffer from diabetes – and even more surprised to learn that it can be controlled in the same way as diabetes in the human. In the more common form, diabetes mellitus, excessive glucose in the bloodstream cannot be utilised by the body due to a lack of insulin. Symptoms are increased hunger and thirst, increased urination, both in quantity and frequency, and/or weight loss.

Treatment, as with human diabetics, is injection with insulin. Owners will be taught how to inject their cats, if they feel capable of doing so. Daily urine testing (which is not as difficult as it sounds, see **urine sample**) is also necessary to check the amount of glucose being excreted so that the amount of insulin given can be adjusted as required.

Treatment for diabetes in the cat is available and effective but is, of course, lifelong. A committed and loving owner will be able both to prolong their cat's life and ensure it is of good quality.

diarrhoea

A lot of us act like Jewish mommas with our cats. Not feeling well, Tiddles? Then have something delicious to eat! If the problem is diarrhoea, we should resist these impulses. A cat with diarrhoea should not be given anything to eat for 24 hours (8 to 12 hours for kittens). Diarrhoea is the body's way of expelling substances which are irritating the bowels. Let the body get on with it and don't make its job harder by filling up your cat with more food (it was probably overeating that caused the problem in the first place). Ensure that plenty of clean water is available but *do not* give your cat milk which will probably make the problem worse.

There are a number of proprietary medicines available for diarrhoea in the cat. Give one, following directions, if you must. I feel that if the body wants to get rid of something, you should let it, and medicines interfere with this natural process. I would only give diarrhoea medication if my cat looked thoroughly miserable.

After 24 hours, if the diarrhoea has cleared up, you can give your cat a number of small meals of bland foods, such as chicken or fish, mixed with a little cooked rice. Some vets recommend feeding a well-formulated dry food. The total amount fed should not be more than half your cat's normal food intake. Take several days to get back to normal quantities and quality. If, as soon as you give your cat its regular food again the diarrhoea recurs, try changing to a different brand of cat food. There is at least one well-known brand which often seems to cause diarrhoea in susceptible cats.

Veterinary attention should be sought if the diarrhoea does not clear up quickly, if your cat vomits as well, if there is blood in the faeces or vomit, if your cat is listless or is in pain.

diet

The cat's diet could form the basis of an entire book. The cat, being a carnivore, *must* receive its protein from animal sources, unlike a dog which manages very well on vegetable protein. Basic points to remember are:

▷ Cats must have high-quality animal protein in their diet. They need a substance called **taurine**, an amino acid which other mammals can make in their own bodies, but cats cannot. Taurine deficiency occurs when a cat is fed on a vegetarian diet, or if it is fed exclusively on dog food, which does not contain enough taurine for the cat. A cat fed on a diet lacking in taurine will suffer from progressive retinal atrophy and, over a period of years, will go blind.

▷ Offal tends to be over-used by owners home-cooking for their cats, because it is inexpensive and easily available. Offal should not be fed more than once or twice a week, especially liver. Many cats become 'hooked' on liver but, due to its high proportion of vitamin A, it is unsuitable for regular feeding. Too much can lead to hypervitaminosis; distorted bones and lameness in the young cat, massive deposits in the liver and kidneys, stiffness, gum and tooth problems in the older cat.

▷ Fish is a traditional meal for cats although it should not be – a diet composed mainly of fish would not be a healthy or balanced one. Fish should always be cooked because raw fish contains an enzyme, thiaminase, which destroys thiamin, also called vitamin B_1. To cook fish with the minimum of smell, bring it to the boil in a little water in a covered saucepan, then turn off the heat, leaving the fish to cook slowly in the hot water. Serve, after removing bones, with the cooking liquid poured over.

▷ Milk is another traditional food for cats which many would be better off without. A surprising number of cats are allergic to the lactose in milk. If it gives your cat diarrhoea, do not give it milk at all. However, if your cat adores milk, begs for it constantly and you're one of those owners who can deny your cat nothing, try giving it reconstituted dried milk or evaporated milk mixed with water (one-third evaporated milk/ two-thirds water). These liquids may not cause problems. All cats should have constant access to clean, fresh water.

▷ Scraps would not, of course, give your cat a nutritionally balanced diet. However, you can supplement your cat's food with leftovers which will enhance its diet; for example, cooked fat from cutlets or steaks (cats don't suffer from coronary artery disease, as we do, so they will enjoy this and it will do them no harm at all), the skin and dark meat from poultry, leftover pieces of cheese, even a few cooked vegetables, chopped up and added to their food.

▷ Commercially-prepared complete cat foods are specially formulated to provide all the nutrition your cat needs. Canned foods are most popular and come in two basic types; the inexpensive food for everyday feeding and the 'gourmet' or luxury foods, usually packed in small cans and fed as a treat. Also available are semi-moist foods which come in packets, ready for feeding, and dry foods which are inexpensive and very simple to feed.

Most owners rely on commercially-manufactured foods and manufacturers spend millions of pounds each year on testing palatability, digestibility and nutrition (probably in that order). They have teams of feline testers who live in luxury and spend their days eating and having their waste products weighed. In the United Kingdom, you can be sure that any feline food on the supermarket shelves is nutritionally adequate if it is marked as a 'complete' food. A 'complementary' food is just that, and requires the addition of other nutrients.

You can also be sure that the tin does not include horse, pony, kangaroo or whale meat, if the manufacturer belongs to the Pet Food Manufacturers' Association, as do the manufacturers of 95% of the pet food sold in the UK. The animal-based protein which the industry uses comes almost entirely from 'those parts of the carcase that custom and usage dictate are unsuitable for human consumption'. This means that the contents of cans marked, for example, 'with tuna', would have been more likely to have mooed than swum while alive. The meat will be tuna-flavoured but will probably differ little in composition from food which is marked 'with chicken'. So, nutritionally, it does not matter which flavour of food you feed your feline; although your cat will probably appreciate the different flavours and prefer some to others.

Gourmet foods, on the other hand, do contain a large proportion of the named meat, varying from around 25% to nearly 100% according to brand. These gourmet foods have a much higher protein content than everyday foods, so your cat will be satiated by eating much less of them. It is unnecessary to feed your cat this type of food on a regular basis, but, if it makes you both happy, it won't do any harm.

To choose an everyday food for an average, adult cat, study the labels on the cans. Most of these foods have a protein content of around 7½%–8% which is perfectly adequate for an average cat's needs. So select one with that amount of protein or more, a relatively low

Young British Shorthair, its blue colouring
the result of dilution (page 54)

level of ash (minerals) and, ideally, little or no cereal or soy content. Although cereal and soy add protein to the diet, it is a lower quality protein than that contained in meat or fish. Having sorted the cans into groups in this way, you will then discover that the prices can vary by quite a few pence for similar quality foods. It is simply a question of finding a reasonably-priced good-quality food that your cat will eat. The most expensive is not neces- sarily the best, as you will see when you read the labels – you may be paying several pence per tin for advertising. The one which your cat appears to favour is not necessarily the best either – it is simply the one which the manufacturers have made most palatable.

Kittens, pregnant and nursing queens, and cats under stress have a higher nutrient re- quirement than normal. The best quality food must be fed and supplements are usually necessary too. Elderly cats require *less* protein than the average cat and carbohydrate in the form of cooked rice, pasta, potato or bread should be added to their food.

Dry foods are popular due to the ease of serving and the fact that they are relatively inexpensive. A few pieces of dry food added to a cat's diet each day provide excellent exercise for the teeth and may help prevent tartar build-up. However, few cats will increase their liquid intake when eating most dry foods and this can lead to concentrated urine and sometimes urological problems. If you always feed dry food, moisten it with water, stock or gravy, unless it is one of the specially-formulated dry foods which do encourage a cat to drink more. Many vets sell this type of food. See also **appetite**.

dilution   (see page 53)

Dilution affects the way we see colour by making it paler. For example, a blue cat is really a 'dilute black' but the black pigmentation is scattered and reflected by the gene responsible for dilution so that we see it as blue.

disinfectants

The best disinfectant to use in the home where cats are kept is a solution of sodium hypochlorite (household bleach) in water. Many disinfectants are toxic or unpleasant to cats (see also **antiseptics**) and should not be used around them. For example, many cats will avoid using litter trays if they have been washed in pine disinfectant. Litter trays and feeding bowls should only be washed in diluted sodium hypochlorite and water. Strangely enough, some cats become excited by bleach and react in the same way as cats under the influence of catnip. Ensure that cats don't get bleach, even diluted bleach, on

their fur as it will burn their skin, or their tongue if they lick it off.

There are a number of disinfectants available which are specially formulated for use where there are cats. These are often used by catteries and large breeding establishments, as they are safe and effective. These disinfectants are available from vets and by mail order from the manufacturers.

Cats cannot detoxify phenols, cresols or related compounds. It is best to assume a disinfectant is unsafe for use in a catty household until you learn otherwise. Contact with these products can cause diarrhoea or vomiting, convulsions and eventual collapse and death.

Even disinfectants considered relatively safe have caused illness in cats when they have come into contact with them in undiluted form. This can cause depression, dehydration, eye and nose discharges, anorexia and ulcerated skin. It is vital to dilute disinfectants before use.

doctoring

Another word for **neutering** (in the male) or spaying (in the female).

dogs

Traditionally considered enemies, many cats and dogs live together in harmony although it is important that they should be introduced in the correct way (see **introductions**). Where a pecking order is concerned, the cat often uses its speed, manoeuvrability and intelligence to become top cat while the canine is relegated to the position of underdog.

domestic

Although used in a broad sense to denote all small, non-wild cats, 'domestic' is also sometimes used to refer to non-pedigree cats.

dominant

A dominant characteristic is one which can be inherited from only one parent. **Polydactylism** is a good example. A cat with more than the usual number of toes which mates with a normal-toed cat can produce kittens with extra toes.

drinks

It is important for a cat to drink liquids, especially water. Although milk is traditionally given to cats, many are allergic to the lactose in milk, and will suffer diarrhoea. If you feel you must give your cat milk, reconstituted powdered milk and evaporated milk, mixed with twice as much water, will be less likely to result in a tummy upset.

Although water should be available for cats, their owners may never see them drinking it. Yet these same cats will probably drink water from puddles outside. It often encourages cats to drink if water is placed in a very large container, such as a fish bowl. In fact, cats will ignore their water bowls and drink from the fish bowl – and they really are not after the fish. It is just that the large bowl is more like a natural waterhole than the small plastic dish. Also, any chlorine smell from the water will have dispersed as the water has been sitting for several days. Many people keep fishless fishtanks for their cats to drink out of.

If you wish to encourage your cat to drink, make a stock by cooking leftover meat or bones in water. Strain, cool and place in your cat's bowl. This is particularly useful if you want a sick cat to drink. A little glucose or honey added to water can also encourage a cat to drink, as can a little salt added to its food.

drooling

Many cats drool with happiness. This harks back to their earliest pleasurable experience – being fed by their mothers. The pleasure of feeding sent their salivary glands into action and, even in adulthood, pleasure still triggers this reaction. So an owner, stroking her or his cat, may end up soaking wet and with shredded knees. See also **kneading**.

drowning

See **artificial respiration**.

dry shampoos

If your cat is grubby and you cannot face the thought of giving it a bath, try a dry shampoo. They are particularly effective if your cat's fur is a little greasy or sticky.

For a pale-coloured cat, sprinkle talcum powder on the coat, rub in and comb through. Comb out all the talc thoroughly and ensure that none gets into your cat's eyes, nose or mouth. Talc is particularly effective on long-haired cats and Persians going to cat shows regularly receive dry shampoos just beforehand to fluff out their magnificent coats. If possible, use a talcum powder without perfume or additives – some cats are sensitive!

For medium-coloured or dark cats, bran or Fullers' Earth is very effective. Warm the bran – the same product you shake on your cereal in the morning – in an oven and then rub it into your cat's fur. Ensure the bran is warm, not hot, or you will burn your cat. Then brush it out and grease, dirt and dust will brush out with it.

Fullers' Earth is another name for grey cat litter. If it is the type you buy, you can use it to clean your cat's coat. Grind some up (after making sure your cat has not used it for its original purpose first), rub it into its fur, without getting it in eyes, nose or mouth, and brush out thoroughly.

E

ears

Owners of non-pedigree cats may never have to clean their cats' ears during an entire lifetime. Pedigree cats' owners – especially if the cat is of a big-eared breed – may have to clean their cats' ears at least once a week because, as a rule, pedigree cats have more wax in their ears, though no-one knows why this is so. A cotton bud can be used to clean away any excess wax but take care not to push the cotton bud down into the ear canal where it can cause damage. Cotton wool, moistened with vegetable oil, is safer but not as effective.

Scratching of the ears or head-shaking may indicate the presence of ear mites, tiny insects which irritate the ear. If you suspect the presence of ear mites, don't try cleaning the ears or treating them yourself. Ear scratching can also be a sign of excess ear wax, which has caused a blockage. Some owners insist on treating ear problems themselves, often with 'canker powder' which, in most cases, will probably make the problem worse. Your vet will treat the specific problem and be far more effective. Consult your vet if your cat's ears smell, are reddened inside or have a brown, waxy discharge.

If your cat has white fur, protect its ear-tips on sunny days with zinc and castor oil ointment as, otherwise, they can burn. The fur is thin on a cat's ear-tips and those with white fur have vulnerable pink skin underneath.

They are prone to sunburn or even skin cancer. See also **deafness**.

eating

See **appetite** and **diet**.

eating disorders

The best-known example of feline eating disorder is the fabric-eating cat. These cats (usually Siamese) eat their owners' woollens, tea-towels, carpets and sometimes even soft furnishings, in fact, any type of fabric they can get their teeth into. At first it was thought that these cats ate fabric because they had been weaned too early; now it is thought that they are probably trying to add fibre to their diet. A cat living wild would obtain roughage from its prey as it would eat fur, feather, bone and gristle. Our pet cats miss out on all that roughage because we feed them soft, processed foods. So if your cat is a fabric-eater you could try adding bran to its meals – a teaspoonful at first, working up to a dessert-spoonful. Grow some **grass** indoors for your cat and add toast, bread crusts and chopped cooked vegetables to its food.

One theory has it that some cats eat wool as a source of lanolin. A queen's nipples exude a lanolin-type substance which keeps them soft and pliable and, so the theory goes, some cats crave a lanolin substitute (although it has to be said that cats will eat fabrics which don't contain lanolin). Buy some pure lanolin from a chemist and add a little to your cat's food to see if this modifies its behaviour.

Fabric-eating cats may just be bored, behaving in the same way as bored humans who will have a meal or a cigarette they don't really want for the sake of something to do. Try to have a regular daily **play** session with your cat and, if you have to be out for a large part of the day, consider providing your cat with a feline playmate.

Anorexia sometimes occurs in cats and a vet should be consulted. Poor appetite is often helped by adding a specially-formulated B vitamin supplement to the diet; it is available from vets and specialist cat suppliers.

Over-eating is usually more of a problem than under-eating where cats are concerned. If you have a fat cat there is only one solution – feed it less. If this makes you feel guilty, you might try feeding the cat more meals per day but with less food being given in the course of a day than before. Remember to alert all friends and neighbours to the fact that your cat is on a diet and tell them they must not give your cat any food at all. Cats are accomplished beggars (and actors) and know how to wheedle a meal out of almost anyone.

eclampsia

Eclampsia, also known as lactational tetany, occurs when a queen has been feeding kittens and her calcium level falls. Symptoms include twitching, leg weakness, panting, vomiting, convulsions and loss of consciousness. Immediate veterinary attention is essential. The queen will be given a calcium injection and recover rapidly. Calcium supplements will be prescribed to prevent the problem recurring.

eczema

This name is loosely used to cover a great variety of skin complaints. Eczema can give skin a dry, scaly appearance, causing your cat to scratch violently, or it can have a wet, red appearance. There are many causes of eczema, the most common one being an allergic reaction to flea saliva. Other causes can be hormone imbalance due to neutering, or an unbalanced diet, for example, feeding too much fish. An allergy to substances in the home can cause eczema and so can skin disease. Veterinary attention is needed to discover the cause and prescribe the appropriate cure. See also **bald patches**.

Egyptian Mau

See **Oriental Tabby**.

elderly cats

An older cat needs different care from a younger cat. But at what age does a cat become elderly? As with humans, it varies with the individual. Some cats are old at ten years of age (equating to about 60 in human terms) while others only begin to slow down at 20 years of age (a centenarian in human terms). Like humans, it seems that long-lived cats have long-lived offspring. The average lifespan for a cat is around 14 to 15 years of age but many live much longer – the oldest cat known reached almost 34½ years of age.

Decide when your cat can be considered 'elderly' by observation and take steps to make its life more comfortable. You will notice it begin to slow down. It may want to sleep more and stay indoors by the fire for longer periods. It may have less patience with children, or noise, or it may become more dependent on you. It may eat less, but more often, drink more, and sometimes be unable to reach its litter tray in time.

This last problem is one where owners frequently consult me. 'My cat has become dirty,' they say. 'What can we do?'

The first thing to realise is that their elderly cat has not become 'dirty'. It simply has less control over its ageing muscles and has not been able to get outside or to its tray in time. The cat will be quite as distressed at its lack of control as its owners. Many of these owners then add to their cat's distress by shouting at it, or locking it out of doors in all weathers. The only way to deal with this problem is with understanding. Provide not just one litter tray, but two – one upstairs and one downstairs if you have a two-storey house. Clean up the occasional accident philosophically – it really can't be helped.

Older cats may have difficulty grooming themselves as well as they once did; stiffening joints will make it harder for them to curl round and groom their backs and hindquarters. Comb or brush your cat regularly and it will look and feel better. Combing or brushing will also reduce the risk of ingesting fur which may form into **hairballs** which the older cat has difficulty in expelling.

Joint stiffness may also make it difficult for an elderly cat to walk upstairs, so ensure its bed is in an accessible place on the ground floor. Food and water bowls could also be placed on a low platform, or upturned box if it is firm, to allow your cat to eat and drink without having to bend too far.

Veterinary checkups should be a regular feature of the older cat's life. Yearly booster vaccinations against cat 'flu and **enteritis** should be continued and this gives your vet an opportunity to check your cat's state of health. Teeth will be inspected as **tartar** often builds up, causing pain which will make your cat reluctant to eat (see **teeth**).

Sometimes the **dewclaw** will overgrow, forming a circle and penetrating the flesh of the cat's leg. It can be difficult to tell which

end should be cut; if in doubt, seek veterinary advice.

Eye or ear function may deteriorate over the years, in which case your cat should be encouraged to remain indoors, or at least spend most of its time indoors. Cats should never be put out at night and this is doubly true of the elderly cat. Nor should they be expected to go out of doors in the cold or wet to relieve themselves; provide a litter tray.

The older cat will appreciate and need additional heat, so a warm, draught-free bed is essential.

Routine is important to cats, especially the elderly. Try to keep to a routine in feeding, grooming and other care needs. Older cats are often unable to adapt to the stress of boarding catteries at holiday times, especially if they have not been in one before. Ask a neighbour to come in to feed your cat instead.

Older cats may begin to put on weight, so guard against this. Provide small meals, more frequently. The older cat requires less protein in its diet too, so the addition of cooked pasta, rice, potato or bread to your cat's meal will have a beneficial effect. Protein makes your cat's kidneys work hard and kidney disease is a scourge of older cats. Constipation may become a problem and a little bran added to your cat's food will help. Special prescription diets, formulated for the needs of the older cat, are available from vets.

However, many older cats live long and healthy lives with just a little modification to their diets and lifestyle, continuing to give their owners love and companionship for many years.

electric shock

Kittens often receive severe injury when they chew electrical flex and can be knocked unconscious. If this occurs, carefully ensure the cat or kitten is no longer in contact with the electrical source. If it is, remove it with something which does not conduct electricity, such as a wooden stick or spoon. Lay the animal on its side and place your hand on the ribs. Place your other hand on top of that and press down gently; releasing immediately. Repeat 15 times per minute. Seek veterinary attention as soon as the cat or kitten has regained consciousness.

It is far easier to prevent this sort of accident than cure the damage afterwards. Remember that kittens chew wires, so keep them out of reach when possible; unplug all electrical appliances when not being used or when you are not in the room to supervise your kitten.

Elizabethan collar

Named after the ruff worn around the neck by the fashion-conscious in the time of Queen Elizabeth I, this is a large, sloping collar which prevents animals from scratching at or licking an injury. Elizabethan collars can be home-made from stiff card or pliable plastic. To make one, cut a circle from a piece of cardboard. Cut a smaller circle out of the middle, to accommodate the head. Then remove a segment, about one-quarter of the size of the collar. You can put tape over the edge of the inner circle so there are no sharp edges in contact with your cat's neck. Secure the collar with tape. Plastic buckets have sometimes been worn by dogs as home-made Elizabethan collars, but no self-respecting cat has ever been seen with a bucket over its head. Cats are usually miserable when forced to wear an Elizabethan collar but it is better than the alternative of a wound which won't heal because the cat won't let it. Try to take your cat's mind off its 'ruff' by giving it an occasional treat to eat.

enteritis

An inflammation of the bowel with varying degrees of severity. See also **Feline Infectious Enteritis**.

entire

Used to refer to a cat which still retains all its sexual organs, ie a cat which has not been spayed or **neutered**.

epilepsy

This is not a common problem in the cat. Anti-epileptic drugs are available from vets if the fits are frequent or serious enough to warrant it. For what to do during an epileptic fit, see **fits**.

euthanasia

Euthanasia – also referred to as 'putting down' or 'putting to sleep' – is usually carried out by giving a painless injection of an overdose of barbiturates. It is the same type of injection that a pet receives to anaesthetise it for surgery, but in a larger dose. Cardiac arrest will occur in 15 seconds without the pet having felt any pain or apprehension.

Many vets prefer owners *not* to be present when euthanasia is carried out. They believe that a pet will fight the drowsiness to respond to their owner's presence and they may be disturbed by their owner's grief and upset. Owners who have stayed with their pets have been further upset by the fact that their pet has thrashed around after the injection was administered. This, however, is not a sign of pain but an effect of the drug, which occasionally causes a jerking of the legs.

When should you contemplate euthanasia for your pet? Don't be afraid to ask your vet's advice on this as no vet will recommend euthanasia except when he or she sees it as

Blue and White Exotic Shorthair kitten, with Blue Persian kitten behind

the only alternative to continued pain and suffering. You should consider euthanasia if:

▷ your cat is suffering from an incurable disease, where its pain or distress cannot be alleviated
▷ its life is no longer worth living because of the ravages of old age, serious physical injuries or disease
▷ your cat is carrying an untreatable disease, such as **Feline Leukaemia Virus**, which can be passed on to other cats.

Grief is, not surprisingly, suffered by most owners when they have taken a decision to have their pet put down. The death of a pet can have an overwhelming effect and mourn-ing can last for many months; this is not made easier by the fact that friends and family often fail to understand the depth of grief being experienced. And what few owners are pre-pared for are the feelings of guilt associated with euthanasia. An owner, no matter how kind and caring, will always wonder 'could I have done more?' Guilt is natural and is part of the recovery process. It is important to remember that few animals – wild or domes-tic – ever die of old age. There will be times when agreeing to euthanasia is the best thing we can do for our pets.

exemption show

Cat clubs hold shows under licence from one of the registration organisations. Before they are permitted to hold a **Championship Show**, they must hold a number of exemption shows. At an exemption show, no **challenge certificates** are awarded.

Exotic Shorthair   *(see opposite)*

These are **Persians** with a haircut, ideal for anyone who likes the Persian temperament but has not got the time to give the daily grooming that a Persian needs. The Exotic Shorthair has been bred from longhairs crossed with shorthairs or **Burmese**. As they usually retain the characteristics of both sets of ancestors, they are affectionate, loyal pets.

They have the shorter snub noses of the Persian, with broad faces and a **cobby** body. Their fur is short, soft and luxurious. Grooming is relatively simple and the coat will not mat.

Bred in a wide variety of colours, the Exotic Shorthair is a strong and healthy breed with the Persian's attractive temperament.

experimental

New breeds of cat are still being developed in a number of ways. Two established breeds may be crossed (for example the **Burmese** and **Chinchilla** to produce the **Burmilla**) or a natural mutation may occur and be developed (as in the **Scottish Fold**). The resulting progeny are described as experimental until they are recognised by a registration organisation.

eyes

Healthy eyes will not need more than an occasional wipe with a dampened piece of cotton wool. A few breeds of cat, most notably the Persians, suffer runny eyes due to blocked tear ducts.

When the discharge is not clear but cloudy, an infection may be the cause. Conjunctivitis, an inflammation of the eyelid lining, is an extremely common problem and can be caused by injury from other cats, twig scratches, foreign bodies in the eye, allergies and irritations. Conjunctivitis may be treated with eye drops or ointment and the cat kept out of the sunlight. Tumours can cause a cat to squint and cataracts cause the pupil to cloud over. For any of these problems, or anything unusual in the eye area, veterinary attention should be sought immediately. Don't try to treat eye problems yourself and only apply eye ointment on veterinary advice.

Delay in seeking advice can result in the loss of an eye. Although many one-eyed cats manage very well, living life to the full, no chances should be taken with eye problems. Should an eye become dislocated from its socket, perhaps as a result of an accident, keep the eye wet with lukewarm water and take the cat to your vet – don't try to replace the eyeball yourself.

Some cats become blind through accident, illness or advancing age and can cope well as long as they live in a stable environment. Some still manage to catch birds.

If the **third eyelid** is visible in the corner of the eyes this can be a symptom of a developing illness.

F

falls

It is said that cats always fall on their feet. They do – and they fall on their chins too. Vets often have to repair cats with damaged legs, pelvises, jaws and teeth, caused when a falling cat comes to a sudden halt on its feet, rocking forward with the momentum of its fall, causing its chin to hit the ground.

A cat has fallen 18 storeys on to concrete and survived, as has a cat falling 20 storeys on to bushes. Yet many cats have been killed falling shorter distances. A kitten can be killed by a fall of less than a metre if it falls awkwardly. It is thought the reason that cats have survived falls from a great height is that they have time to adopt an aerodynamic position, spreading out their limbs to take advantage of the cushion of air beneath the body: in effect, flying.

Many owners believe that cats do not fall and leave upstairs windows wide open. But a cat, chasing a fly and lost in the excitement of the chase, will follow it straight out of the window. A cat, basking in sunshine on the windowsill, may turn over in its sleep and roll off. So keep windows closed, or open just an inch or two, or cover wide-open windows with a wire mesh screen.

false pregnancy

False pregnancy can occur in the cat when a queen feels she is pregnant even when she is not. The queen will go off call for the nine weeks that a normal pregnancy would last, during which time she will be blissfully happy. So will most owners, who will be glad of nine weeks' peace and quiet. The queen may make a nest and may even come into milk.

In some cases, no reason for the false pregnancy can be discovered, except for wishful thinking on the part of the cat. In others, the queen may well have been 'mated' even if the owner has no entire male in the household. Not many people know this, but neutered males occasionally mate unspayed females. (I have a neutered male who has been known to climb on top of my breeding queen when she is calling. Once on top he realises he doesn't know what to do next and dismounts with a foolish expression on his face.) Some neutered males *do* know what to do next and a form of mating takes place, although there is no chance of the female becoming pregnant. A cat will ovulate in response to penetration and a false pregnancy can follow, but without any kittens nine weeks later.

Breeders who want their queen to have a rest between litters, without giving their cat the contraceptive pill, have been known to make use of a neutered tom in this way.

fasting

Fasting, for both animals and humans, has

fallen from popularity in recent times. Yet in its natural state, the cat would be obliged to fast frequently – on those days when it caught nothing to eat. Fasting allows the digestive system to cleanse itself of impurities and gives the organs a chance to rest. Virtually every well cared for pet cat in the western world could afford to lose a little weight and fasting uses up fat stored in the body. Cats instinctively eat when food is available to store up for the times when it is not. For pet cats, food is usually always available, so any excess fat stores are never used up.

If fasting your cat, choose one day a week for the fast and make it a regular routine. Your cat should be given nothing at all to eat, no titbits or treats, and no milk, for 24 hours. Water, or water with honey or glucose should be available at all times. Fast day is a good time to clean your cat's teeth (see **teeth**) because fasting may cause a film to form on the teeth as toxins are eliminated from the system.

Most cats adapt well to fasting. Greedy cats which are always crying for food will cry no more or less than usual on fast day and non-greedy cats accept the situation with equanimity. If your cat goes outdoors, instruct your neighbours not to feed your cat on the fast day each week as many cats will rush straight round to the neighbour's house to plead pitifully for food. On the day after the fast, feed the usual amount, but split into at least two meals.

fault

What is a fault in one breed is not necessarily a fault in another. Each breed has its own **standard of points**, which is a description of what a member of that breed should look like. If a cat deviates in looks from that standard of points, that deviation is a fault. For example, a long nose would be a fault in a **Persian** but not in a **Siamese**.

feeding

See **appetite** and **diet**.

Feline Dysautonomia

This is an illness which interferes with the functioning of a cat's autonomic nervous system, which regulates the internal organs, such as the heart and lungs, as well as the glands.

▷ transmission: at the time of writing the method of transmission is not known
▷ symptoms: dilated pupils (no reaction to light changes), avoidance of bright light, constipation, dilation of the oesophagus, lack of appetite, vomiting
▷ treatment: symptoms can be alleviated although no cure is currently possible. Eye drops will overcome dilation of the pupils, fluids can be fed to prevent dehydration and liquid paraffin can be given to combat constipation
▷ notes: This illness was first discovered in 1981 and was originally called Key-Gaskell syndrome after the two men who first described it. The recovery rate is very low, possibly as low as 10%. Feline Dysautonomia cannot be passed on to humans.

Feline Immunodeficiency Virus (FIV)

FIV, like **FeLV**, causes a disease in cats similar to AIDS in humans.

▷ transmission: FIV appears to be transmitted in saliva, via bite wounds
▷ symptoms: similar to FeLV – anaemia, loss of weight, vomiting, diarrhoea, weakness
▷ treatment: none at present. Some cats

with the virus have lived for more than five years but should be kept indoors, away from other cats, to prevent them transmitting the disease. If this is not possible, euthanasia should be considered

▷ notes: this disease was discovered in 1987 although it had probably been in existence for many years without being identified. It was, at first, called Feline T-lymphotropic Lentivirus (FTLV) because of its similarity to FeLV, although the two viruses are not related. FIV cannot be transmitted to humans.

Feline Infectious Anaemia (FIA)

A particularly dangerous disease because the symptoms are often extremely difficult to spot.

▷ transmission: by fleas and other bloodsucking insects which spread the parasite, *Haemobartonella felis*; kittens in the womb can be infected via the placenta

▷ symptoms: listlessness, loss of appetite, loss of weight, weakness, pale gums, sometimes slight jaundice; in some cases symptoms are so mild as to be unnoticeable

▷ treatment: blood transfusion in severe cases; organic iron compounds, antibiotics, drugs to kill the parasites. For kittens born with FIA, euthanasia is the only course of action

▷ prevention: eradication of all blood-sucking parasites

▷ notes: many cats may suffer from FIA without showing any signs, until stress or a second infection make the cat obviously ill. Many cats with **FeLV**

develop FIA as their immune system is depressed; the outlook is not good for cats with both diseases.

Feline Infectious Enteritis (FIE or Panleucopaenia)

Although almost always fatal, FIE is entirely preventable.

▷ transmission: the virus is shed in urine, faeces, saliva and vomit and can persist in the environment for up to a year

▷ symptoms: high temperature, sunken eyes, withdrawal – the cat will seek seclusion, painful abdomen, vomiting of a greenish liquid, dehydration – the cat may appear to want to drink but be unable to

▷ treatment: antibiotics, intravenous fluids, blood transfusions in serious cases

▷ prevention: vaccination at nine weeks, twelve weeks and thereafter yearly boosters; the vaccine is given combined with vaccine for **Feline Respiratory Disease** (cat 'flu)

▷ notes: FIE can be an extremely severe and quick-acting illness. If symptoms are spotted, immediate veterinary attention is essential. The mortality rate of cats contracting this disease can be as much as 100% yet the disease is preventable with yearly vaccination. Affected cats require enormous efforts from their owners in nursing care: TLC can make the difference between life and death.

Feline Infectious Peritonitis (FIP)

A disease of young cats for which there is no cure.

▷ transmission: a virus transmitted by direct contact; it cannot live long outside the body

▷ symptoms: fever, lack of appetite, loss of weight, withdrawal, vomiting, diarrhoea, swollen abdomen

▷ treatment: FIP is invariably fatal but life can be prolonged with antibiotics, treatment for dehydration and vitamin supplements. However, once a cat refuses to eat, little can be done to prolong its life. Euthanasia should be considered

▷ prevention: no vaccine exists. In a household where a cat has suffered from FIP, no other cat should be introduced for a month, at least

▷ notes: FIP usually affects young cats, under five years of age, and exists in two forms: wet FIP with fluid accumulation in the abdomen and chest and dry FIP with enlargement of various organs; everything else about the disease is similar.

Feline Leukaemia Virus (FeLV)

The outlook for a cat with Feline Leukaemia Virus is not good.

▷ transmission: the disease is believed to be transmitted in the saliva, by biting, licking or sneezing

▷ symptoms: lack of appetite, weight loss, fever, general malaise, swollen glands, blood in faeces

▷ treatment: no cure at present. Cats with the virus should be isolated from other cats. Euthanasia may have to be considered

▷ prevention: FeLV vaccines are now available in the United Kingdom and are said to give up to 97.5% of all

vaccinated cats immunity to the disease. Your vet may suggest a blood test (or even two) before immunisation to ensure your cat is testing negative for FeLV. Vaccinations are given at nine weeks and twelve weeks; thereafter yearly boosters are given

▷ notes: FeLV suppresses a cat's immune system, making it more vulnerable to other diseases, in the same way that AIDS suppresses the human immune system. FeLV has consequently been called 'the cats' AIDS', sometimes leading to widespread panic. Human beings *cannot* catch AIDS (or leukaemia) from a cat suffering from FeLV.

Feline Respiratory Disease (FRD)

This is usually referred to as cat 'flu although it is much more serious for a cat than 'flu usually is for a human. FRD is caused by a number of different viruses but in about 80% of cases two viruses are responsible for this inflammation of the cat's upper respiratory system – feline viral rhinotracheitis (FVR) and feline calici-virus (FCV). Of the two, FVR infections are usually more severe.

▷ transmission: contact with an infected cat. Sneezes are a common way for FRD to be transmitted as infected droplets are showered over other cats

▷ symptoms: sneezing, runny eyes and nose, lack of appetite, breathing difficulties

▷ treatment: antibiotics for secondary bacterial infections, eye ointments or drops, vitamins and possibly treatment for dehydration. An owner's Tender Loving Care in the home nursing of a cat suffering from FRD will make an enormous difference in its recovery, as many become so miserable they lose the will to live. Keep your cat warm and comfortable. Clean away mucus from nose and eyes with dampened cotton wool and smear nose and under the eyes with a little petroleum jelly. Groom your cat to help it feel better. Try to make it purr – this can relieve difficult breathing. A vapour bath can help your cat's breathing if it does not object. Take it into the bathroom with you when you are having a bath or shower and add a little Vicks vapour rub to water. Try to persuade your cat to eat by giving it strong-smelling foods which you have warmed to blood heat

▷ prevention: FRD is easily prevented by means of a yearly **inoculation**. Large concentrations of cats pose a risk; if using a holiday cattery, ensure it is one where inoculation certificates are insisted upon and that there are impermeable sneeze barriers between the cats' runs. If you know someone who has a sneezing cat, don't let them even touch *your* cat. At the vet's keep your cat in the car until it is your turn to be seen if you can safely do so; vets' waiting rooms often contain sneezing cats

▷ notes: as always, prevention is easier – and cheaper – than cure.

Feline T-lymphotropic Lentivirus (FTLV)

See **Feline Immunodeficiency Virus (FIV)**.

Feline Urological (or Urolithiasis) Syndrome (FUS)

FUS is caused by the formation of 'stones' in the bladder. These are formed from a gritty sludge in the urine which can block the ureter, the tube which joins the kidney to the bladder. This is a particular problem in the male, where the passage is very narrow, and it can cause an emergency. If you suspect your cat, male *or* female, is suffering from FUS, you must take it to the vet at once – without *immediate* attention it could die.

▷ symptoms: urinating on carpets or furniture, straining on the litter tray or spending a long time on the litter tray, constant licking of the penis or tail area (penis may be visible and swollen). Symptoms when the bladder becomes blocked include blood in the urine, obvious pain, vomiting, depression, difficulty in walking. Veterinary attention is now extremely urgent

▷ treatment: if the bladder is blocked, surgery is necessary. A fine tube will be passed into the bladder to allow the escape of urine. In less serious cases, the diet should be altered, and foods specifically formulated to deal with FUS are now available from vets. Urine acidifiers may be prescribed

▷ prevention: feed several small meals a day rather than one large one. This controls the pH content of the urine, keeping it more acidic. Encourage your cat to drink, adding a little salt to its diet if it does not drink much. Add liquids to your cat's food. Don't neuter male cats too early – this seems to contribute to the likelihood of your cat developing FUS in later life. Don't feed your cat dry foods which concentrate the urine. Exercise your cat, as this will encourage it to pass urine more frequently. See also **cystitis**.

Feral cats photographed near a slaughterhouse, a good food source (page 68)

FeLV

See **Feline Leukaemia Virus**.

feral   (see page 67)

Feral cats have been born into, or have reverted to, the wild, usually after having been thrown out by their owners. They congregate in groups, which can be as large as 40 or 50 cats, in the environs of hospitals, factories and warehouses. Sprayed urine and cat faeces on a large scale make the feral groups unpopular and can result in their 'landlords' arranging for pest control companies to destroy them. Several charities have alternative methods for the control of feral cats. They trap the cats, neuter them, and return them to the wild. While the cats are anaesthetised, the tip of one ear has a nick cut out of it. This visual sign prevents the same cat being trapped and operated on twice. Some groups are now reappraising the neutering of feral cats as it alters the **hierarchy** within the group. The life expectancy of the average feral cat is around six years.

FIA

See **Feline Infectious Anaemia**.

FIE

See **Feline Infectious Enteritis**.

FIP

See **Feline Infectious Peritonitis**.

fish

Fish is a traditional food for cats, although it is far from being a balanced diet. It is, however, an excellent source of protein. It should always be cooked as raw fish contains an enzyme, thiaminase, which inactivates thiamin (vitamin B_1) and makes less of the vitamin available from other foods. To cook fish without smell, bring it to the boil in a little water or milk in a covered saucepan then turn off the heat. Leave to poach in its own heat for ten minutes. Serve the cooled fish and the fish skin (a good source of roughage) with bones removed and a little of the liquid poured over it. Or pour the liquid over cereal and serve as a separate meal. White fish and oily fish are nutritious but neither contains all the nutrients cats need, so should not be fed exclusively. Some cats, fed nothing but fish over a period of years, have become extremely ill, unable to walk and in great pain. They recovered when their diets were improved and vitamin supplements added. Although many owners like to give their cat an occasional treat by giving them some freshly cooked fish, a canned cat food would be more nutritious, probably more palatable, and certainly a lot cheaper.

fits

A fit will lead to a loss of consciousness which may last a few seconds to several minutes. During a fit, a cat may rush around in a dazed manner, foam at the mouth, become incontinent and its limbs may jerk uncontrollably.

If your cat is having a fit

▷ contact your vet immediately
▷ ensure your cat is in a safe, warm and comfortable place. If your cat wears a collar, remove it. Keep the room quiet and dark
▷ keep your cat under observation but do not touch it, unless you must for reasons of safety
▷ if the fit passes before the vet arrives, keep your cat warm, quiet and comfortable. Cats may become incontinent during a fit, or foam at the

mouth; you can wipe this up once the fit has passed.

Reasons for fits include poisoning, epilepsy, head injuries and infections such as **Feline Infectious Peritonitis** or **rabies**. A queen with kittens may have a fit as a result of **eclampsia** and, rarely, a kitten may have a fit due to worms or teething.

FIV

See **Feline Immunodeficiency Virus**.

flatulence

Flatulence – wind – is never well tolerated by anyone on the receiving end. There are steps you can take to lessen the problem.

Flatulence can be caused by a bowel infection, in which case your vet will supply antibiotics which will clear the problem. But the likeliest cause of flatulence is the food you are feeding your cat.

▷ Are you feeding your cat peas or beans or other vegetables? If so, stop!

▷ Are you feeding your cat meat which is not completely fresh? Or are you feeding liver or carbohydrate? If so, change its diet.

▷ Are you feeding your cat a food which is very high in protein? If it is not absorbing all the protein, this may lead to flatulence. You could try adding a little bran, for roughage, to the food.

▷ If you are feeding canned cat food, try changing the brand. Some produce more gas than others.

▷ If your cat is elderly, its muscle tone and control will be poor. Try improving its diet while feeding it less protein, ensuring it is regularly wormed and giving a vitamin/mineral supplement on veterinary advice.

▷ Try mixing activated charcoal with your cat's food. This often helps – if your cat will accept it.

fleas

When grooming your cat each week, look for the presence of fleas. You might notice black, dusty specks in the fur; these are flea droppings. Because they contain undigested blood (your cat's) they will turn red if combed out and dampened with water. You might see a flea, a tiny reddish-brown insect, but you are more likely to see their droppings, particularly around the chin, ears and tail. By the time you see your cat scratching there are likely to be many fleas present.

Every cat will have fleas at some time in its life; some will attract fleas every few months. There is no need to be embarrassed because your cat has fleas, as long as you treat them as soon as you notice them. The comfortable lifestyle most people enjoy makes life more comfortable for fleas too and they thrive in warm, well-furnished and carpeted surroundings.

To eradicate fleas, you must treat your cat *and* your home at the same time. Fleas live on your cat for part of their life cycle but they breed in carpets and furniture. When the young hatch, they hop aboard your cat for a meal. If you treat your cat's fleas but don't kill those in your home, your cat will quickly become infested again.

Sprays are most widely used for the eradication of fleas and these are available from pet stores and veterinary surgeries. Follow instructions to the letter and always remember you are dealing with toxic substances – they have to be in order to kill fleas. Hold your cat firmly but gently by the scruff and spray a two to three second burst along your cat's back and the same along its tummy. It is unnecessary to cover every inch of fur – two swift bursts will get rid of the fleas. Be careful not to spray over your cat's face and don't breathe in the spray. If you can, spray your cat out of doors so the breeze blows away any excess spray. Wear rubber gloves, or scrub your hands and arms thoroughly after spraying. If spraying indoors, don't spray in the same room as your cat's food or water dishes, or in a room where there is a fish tank as it can kill the fish.

Then spray your home, using an environment spray, again following the instructions on the can. The edges of carpets, especially near sources of heat, should be sprayed, as should sofas, chairs and beds on which your cat sits or lies. Never use this type of flea spray on your cat.

Some people find powders easier to use on their cats. Powders should be sprinkled on, keeping away from the cat's face, and then thoroughly brushed out. A cat which hates flea treatments can be placed in an old pillowcase, completely covered up to its neck with just its head sticking out. Place the powder inside the pillowcase and rub it into the fur through the fabric. Alternatively, there is a type of applicator brush for the powder which has hollow spikes. Brushed with this applicator, the powder is distributed throughout the cat's fur.

Flea collars release powdered insecticide which spreads gradually over a cat's coat. It takes several days for the insecticide to get to work, during which time fleas will continue to irritate the cat. If you use a flea collar on your cat you should remove it for several hours every day to allow your cat's skin to breathe. It should always be removed if it becomes wet. Ensure that the collar's insecticide is compatible with any environment spray you might use and bear in mind that, if you have successfully rid the environment of fleas, your cat is being exposed to an unnecessary amount of insecticide. An RSPCA survey showed that from a sample of 569 cats, 161 were injured or died through wearing flea collars and 408 suffered from dermatitis around the neck.

There are a number of 'green' flea products available which use herbal repellents. These, although safer for your cat, will only repel fleas, not kill them. Herbal flea collars and lotions have a limited effectiveness. Wormwood (*Artemisia absinthium*) is a perennial herb which can be grown in pots on the windowsill or in the garden and yields a bitter oil which repels fleas. Dried and crushed leaves can be rubbed into your cat's coat then thoroughly brushed out, and cotton bags of the dried leaves can be placed in your cat's bed to keep it flea-free.

Feeding garlic to a cat is also reputed to repel fleas, as well as discouraging intestinal worms. The theory is that the scent of the garlic is exuded by the cat's pores and is a disincentive for a flea to bite it!

▷ Warning: don't use different types of flea or insect repellent product together as, combined, they can be extremely toxic. And don't worm your cat for at least 5 days before or after a flea treatment; the two treatments combined can be toxic.

flehmen response

The flehmen response is seen in a cat which is worried or nervous. It will gasp and inhale air through its open mouth. At the back of the mouth is the **Jacobson's organ** which enables a cat to taste and smell at the same time. The cat is using this organ to collate information about everything which is happening around it.

Two Foreign White kittens with two Seal-Point Siamese

'flu

See **Feline Respiratory Disease**.

Foreign   (see above)

The Foreign cat's slim, sleek looks give the clue to its **Siamese** forebears. It shares a common ancestry but, where the Siamese has been bred with coloured points, the Foreigns are one colour all over (self-coloured). In the United Kingdom the patterned version of this cat is called the Oriental and the chocolate-coloured version is known as the **Havana**. In every country but the United Kingdom, the Foreign is known as the Oriental.

These cats also resemble the Siamese in temperament, although they tend to be a little quieter. They can be demanding of their owners but know how to get their own way quietly but firmly. They take great joy in life and are tremendous characters, being very responsive to their owners. They are ideal cats for someone who will allow them free range for their active and agile temperaments. They love company – human and feline – so do need companions.

They are easy to groom and **hand grooming** will keep these attractive cats looking their best. The best-known of the available colours are the Foreign White, Foreign Lilac, Foreign Black and Foreign Blue.

71

Foreign Longhair

See **Angora**.

foreign type

Used to describe a body shape and not an origin. A foreign type of cat has long, slim legs and body, a whip-like tail and a wedge-shaped face. They share a temperament too; being active, agile, highly-intelligent and mischievous. The most popular of the foreign type of cat is the **Siamese**. Cornish and Devon **Rexes**, although bred from British stock, are considered to be of foreign type, even in the United Kingdom.

Forest Cat

See **Norwegian Forest Cat**.

foster mothers

See **adoption of kittens by a cat**.

fourteen-day rule

The fourteen-day rule is observed by those registration organisations that hold cat shows.

It means that no cat can be shown more than once every fourteen days. In fact, if a cat is present at a show, no other cat from *that household* can be taken to a show within a fourteen-day period. The idea behind the rule is not just to reduce stress on the cat – because attending a cat show is stressful – but also to inhibit the spread of disease. If a cat has picked up an infection at a show, signs of the infection will become noticeable within fourteen days. It will not then be taken to a subsequent show where it would pass on infection to other cats.

FRD

See **Feline Respiratory Disease**.

frost

The American word for the fur colour lilac.

furballs

See **hairballs**.

FUS

See **Feline Urological Syndrome**.

G

gauntlets

The white feet of some breeds which have darker-coloured legs. Gauntlets are longer than **mitts** or **gloves**. For example, the **Birman** has white gauntlets on its back legs which cover the paw entirely and go up the back of the hock.

GCCF

See **Governing Council of the Cat Fancy**.

German Rex

See **Rex**.

gestation   (see page 74)

The length of pregnancy, or gestation, in the domestic cat is around 63 days. Some pregnancies last 64, 65 or 66 days; few last less than 63 days. Kittens born before day 56 are unlikely to survive.

A pregnant queen will often 'pink up' between 2½ to 3 weeks after mating, that is, her nipples will turn pink and become slightly swollen. A cat which has already had one litter, however, may not pink up noticeably.

Queens during this time will often become very affectionate, wanting to spend a lot of time on their owners' laps. They may sleep more than usual and their appetite will increase. A pregnant queen should be allowed to eat as much good-quality food as she wishes.

Miscarriage in the cat is not particularly common but it does sometimes occur so care should be taken that the queen is not confronted by aggressive cats or dogs, especially in the latter part of the pregnancy, nor should she be encouraged to climb or jump. Be particularly careful about the use of any toxic substance, including flea spray. If the queen has fleas, telephone your vet for advice before using any flea product on her, especially during the early stages of pregnancy. Also be particularly careful about the use of disinfectants, household cleaners, carpet shampoos and any other product which might have a toxic effect. If you were planning a spring-clean, wait until after the kittens are born and, ideally, until after the they have gone to their new homes.

The table overleaf will help you work out the date on which your cat is likely to have her kittens. Look at the dates on the left of each double column for the date mating took place. The expected birth date is the date on the right of each double column. This table, which assumes a gestation period of 64 days, is of course most helpful to people with pedigree cats where mating is carefully arranged and supervised. Moggy owners, and that's most of us, may not realise kittens are on the way until the pregnancy is well advanced. See **pinking up** and **season** for clues to give you some idea of when the kittens may be due.

Jan	Mar	Feb	Apr	Mar	May	Apr	Jun	May	Jul	Jun	Aug
1	6	1	6	1	4	1	4	1	4	1	4
2	7	2	7	2	5	2	5	2	5	2	5
3	8	3	8	3	6	3	6	3	6	3	6
4	9	4	9	4	7	4	7	4	7	4	7
5	10	5	10	5	8	5	8	5	8	5	8
6	11	6	11	6	9	6	9	6	9	6	9
7	12	7	12	7	10	7	10	7	10	7	10
8	13	8	13	8	11	8	11	8	11	8	11
9	14	9	14	9	12	9	12	9	12	9	12
10	15	10	15	10	13	10	13	10	13	10	13
11	16	11	16	11	14	11	14	11	14	11	14
12	17	12	17	12	15	12	15	12	15	12	15
13	18	13	18	13	16	13	16	13	16	13	16
14	19	14	19	14	17	14	17	14	17	14	17
15	20	15	20	15	18	15	18	15	18	15	18
16	21	16	21	16	19	16	19	16	19	16	19
17	22	17	22	17	20	17	20	17	20	17	20
18	23	18	23	18	21	18	21	18	21	18	21
19	24	19	24	19	22	19	22	19	22	19	22
20	25	20	25	20	23	20	23	20	23	20	23
21	26	21	26	21	24	21	24	21	24	21	24
22	27	22	27	22	25	22	25	22	25	22	25
23	28	23	28	23	26	23	26	23	26	23	26
24	29	24	29	24	27	24	27	24	27	24	27
25	30	25	30	25	28	25	28	25	28	25	28
26	31	26	May 1	26	29	26	29	26	29	26	29
27	Apr 1	27	2	27	30	27	30	27	30	27	30
28	2	28	3	28	31	28	Jul 1	28	31	28	31
29	3			29	Jun 1	29	2	29	Aug 1	29	Sep 1
30	4			30	2	30	3	30	2	30	2
31	5			31	3			31	3		

Jul	Sep	Aug	Oct	Sep	Nov	Oct	Dec	Nov	Jan	Dec	Feb
1	3	1	4	1	4	1	4	1	4	1	3
2	4	2	5	2	5	2	5	2	5	2	4
3	5	3	6	3	6	3	6	3	6	3	5
4	6	4	7	4	7	4	7	4	7	4	6
5	7	5	8	5	8	5	8	5	8	5	7
6	8	6	9	6	9	6	9	6	9	6	8
7	9	7	10	7	10	7	10	7	10	7	9
8	10	8	11	8	11	8	11	8	11	8	10
9	11	9	12	9	12	9	12	9	12	9	11
10	12	10	13	10	13	10	13	10	13	10	12
11	13	11	14	11	14	11	14	11	14	11	13
12	14	12	15	12	15	12	15	12	15	12	14
13	15	13	16	13	16	13	16	13	16	13	15
14	16	14	17	14	17	14	17	14	17	14	16
15	17	15	18	15	18	15	18	15	18	15	17
16	18	16	19	16	19	16	19	16	19	16	18
17	19	17	20	17	20	17	20	17	20	17	19
18	20	18	21	18	21	18	21	18	21	18	20
19	21	19	22	19	22	19	22	19	22	19	21
20	22	20	23	20	23	20	23	20	23	20	22
21	23	21	24	21	24	21	24	21	24	21	23
22	24	22	25	22	25	22	25	22	25	22	24
23	25	23	26	23	26	23	26	23	26	23	25
24	26	24	27	24	27	24	27	24	27	24	26
25	27	25	28	25	28	25	28	25	28	25	27
26	28	26	29	26	29	26	29	26	29	26	28
27	29	27	30	27	30	27	30	27	30	27	Mar 1
28	30	28	31	28	Dec 1	28	31	28	31	28	2
29	Oct 1	29	Nov 1	29	2	29	Jan 1	29	Feb 1	29	3
30	2	30	2	30	3	30	2	30	2	30	4
31	3	31	3			31	3			31	5

Table of probable birth dates (see page 73)

ghost markings

Some kittens are born with ghost tabby markings on their fur which disappears as they mature. This is particularly common with black kittens because black kittens are basically 'double tabbies'. A tabby cat has black stripes on an **agouti** background (seen by us as grey) but a black cat has black stripes on a black background. Burmese kittens often have ghost markings for the first few months of life.

ginger

The gene which produces the ginger colour, known as red in the pedigree world, is sex-linked, and ginger cats are almost always males. Female ginger cats are discovered occasionally but they are likely to be sterile. The gene producing the colour acts like a coat of varnish, colouring the fur but letting you see the pattern below. In the case of the ginger cat, the pattern below is tabby, which is why ginger cats are striped.

gingivitis

Gingivitis, or inflammation of the gums, can occur in kittens when their permanent teeth erupt (around three to seven months) and in adults, especially if **tartar** has accumulated on the teeth, or if they are suffering from vitamin deficiency, kidney disease, or leukaemia.

▷ symptoms: bad breath, difficulty in eating, dribbling, gum pain, sometimes blood-tinged saliva.

▷ treatment: teeth need to be cleaned by a vet (usually under anaesthetic) and/or sometimes removal of a tooth or teeth. If the gingivitis has been caused by an associated condition, treatment of the condition should resolve the problem.

Antibacterial and vitamin therapy may be prescribed.

▷ prevention: if your cat will allow it, clean its teeth once a week (see **teeth**). If not, your vet can descale your cat's teeth once a year.

gloves

The white feet of some breeds which have darker-coloured legs. Gloves are smaller than **gauntlets** and slightly smaller than **mitts**. The **Birman** has gloves on its front paws.

Governing Council of the Cat Fancy (GCCF)

The GCCF is the longest-established and largest registration body for cats in the United Kingdom, equating to the Kennel Club in the dog world. The majority of British cat owners will have little or no contact with any registration organisation; the first and only contact may be when a pedigree kitten is purchased. If it is registered with the GCCF the new owner will have to complete the transfer of ownership form and send it to the GCCF. This officially transfers ownership from the breeder to the new owner. This may be the extent of the new owner's contact with the GCCF unless they decide to start breeding cats, join a cat club, or take their cat to shows.

A breeder whose cats are registered with the GCCF will register her/his kittens when they are born with the GCCF, who will keep a record of them. Many cat shows are held under the rules of the GCCF, who will license the show and appoint the judges officiating at it. Breeds of pedigree cats are 'recognised' by the registration bodies, which means they will accept them as a separate breed of pedigree cat. Cat clubs are affiliated to one registration organisation or another. If they become affiliated to the GCCF and have been in existence for three years and have more than 100 members, they can send an elected delegate to the Council, so helping form policy. Clubs with more than 150 members can send two delegates.

Only the **National Cat Club** can send four delegates to Council, an archaic privilege allowed because the NCC was the first cat club set up in the United Kingdom. Formed in 1887, it started up the first register of cats. In 1898, a rival body, the Cat Club, was set up but the two merged in 1910 and became the Governing Council of the Cat Fancy.

Among the GCCF's many powers are those of discipline; they are able to warn, fine or suspend any member or club who offends against its rules. Their ultimate sanction against a member – suspension – means that that person cannot register their kittens, or show them, or remain a member of an affiliated club. The disciplinary powers of the registration bodies should be borne in mind by anyone who purchases a kitten with which they are not satisfied; if a complaint to the breeder yields no result, a complaint should be made to the registration body concerned.

Since 1983, a second major registration body has been in existence in the United Kingdom. Called the **Cat Association of Britain (CA)**, it fulfils the same functions as the GCCF and recognises several breeds of cats which are not yet recognised by the GCCF.

Grand Champion and Grand Premier

A Grand Champion is an entire cat of either sex which has won the title of **Champion** three times under three different judges. The title is always shortened, on pedigree forms, to Gr Ch.

A Grand Premier (Gr Pr) is a neutered cat which has won the title of Premier three times under three different judges.

grass, green matter

Every cat needs some green matter as an aid to digestion and to help expel **hairballs** or other matter irritating the stomach. Cats can often be seen stripping pieces of grass and swallowing it. Outdoor cats can help themselves to grass and herbs but cats which are kept indoors must have greenstuff specially grown for them.

Although you can grow lawn grass in a tub on the windowsill, cocksfoot grass is considered to be an ideal grass for a cat to nibble. Packets of seed, and ready-planted tubs, are available from specialist cat equipment suppliers. Sow some every couple of weeks in order to have new growth ready as the old is nibbled down.

grooming

All cats benefit from being groomed by their owner at least once a week. Some, such as the **Persians**, need daily grooming or their fur will tangle and matt. How often you comb or brush your cat will depend on the type of fur it has and the time of year. All cats require more grooming in springtime as the spring moult gets under way. This will not only help your cat's health, making the development of **hairballs** less likely, but will also keep your house much tidier! Cats under stress will also moult more and should have extra grooming sessions. Old or sick cats are less able to groom themselves and will appreciate help from their owner.

Start grooming your cat when it is a young kitten, so that it becomes accustomed to it. Begin simply by stroking it, as if your hands were brushes. When it becomes used to this, brush or comb it for short periods. Always start and end a grooming session by grooming the places your cat enjoys, such as under the chin, behind the ears or on the tummy. Then groom the back and tail, and the chest. Turn your cat onto its back to groom this area, and this is easier if you have the cat on your lap. If your cat won't allow this, let it stand upright and comb the belly from each side in turn.

A metal comb is most effective; choose a comb with teeth of equal length for a short-haired cat and a wide-toothed comb with alternate long and short teeth for a longhaired cat. A pure bristle brush will make the coat shine without causing static. Finish off the grooming session with a rubber brush to collect loose hair. At the end of a grooming session some owners of shorthaired breeds rub the cat with a piece of chamois leather to give the coat a shine.

If a coat becomes matted or tangled, deal with this as soon as possible as the tangles will get worse. Cats with very badly matted coats have to be sheared, under anaesthetic, by a vet. Try to unpick small knots with your fingers, as combing them out will hurt your cat. If this does not work, they can be cut out. Use a pair of round-ended scissors; place them below the knot and cut in a direction away from the skin, not towards it. See also **bathing a cat**.

guard hairs

A cat's coat is made up of an undercoat of down hairs and a topcoat of guard hairs, which protects the insulating undercoat. There are two types of guard hair, the awn hairs which have a bristly tip, and the much less numerous primary guard hairs which are coarser. It is these hairs which stand on end when a cat is fighting and wants to make itself look large and threatening. The primary guard hairs may be of a different colour to the rest of the cat. For example, a pure black cat is rare indeed as it will often have some white guard hairs in its coat. Black show cats often have these tweezered out!

H

haemorrhage

See **bleeding, internal** and **bleeding, external**.

hairballs

Cats groom themselves every time they finish eating or drinking, when they want to calm themselves down and when they just feel like it. Their tongues have backward-pointing barbs which act like the teeth of combs and, like those teeth, some loose hair sticks. This is swallowed by the cat and can build up in the stomach into a hairball. Usually, a cat's digestive system can cope with swallowed hair and it will be expelled, either in the faeces or by the cat coughing or vomiting it up. Although this sight can upset some owners it does no harm and the cat should not be treated as if it were 'ill' just because it has got rid of a hairball. It is more a cause for concern if the cat does *not* manage to get rid of the hairball.

A cat with a hairball may be miserable and off its food; it may eat a mouthful or two of food and be unable to eat more because of the blockage, then return to the food soon after, again only able to eat a little. It may make a 'honking' sound, trying to cough up the hairball.

Give the cat a teaspoonful of liquid paraffin once a day for three or four days or until it expels the hairball, if this takes less than four days. Never continue giving liquid paraffin for longer than this as it coats the cat's stomach and intestines, hastening the passage of food through the stomach and so robbing the cat of nourishment. It is not always easy to persuade a cat to take a teaspoonful of liquid paraffin and commercial preparations are available specifically to get rid of hairballs. These are made to be attractive to cats so there will be no argument over taking them. Follow the directions carefully.

Another remedy is petroleum jelly, which can be given by placing a blob on the cat's paw. Cats don't like having greasy paws and will lick it off.

Prevention, as always, is easier than cure. If a cat is combed regularly (once a week as a rule and two or three times a week during the moulting season in spring) hairballs should not be a problem. Feeding your cat an oily fish, such as tinned sardines or mackerel, once a week will also help ease through any swallowed hair.

halitosis

See **bad breath**.

hand grooming

Some of the shorthaired breeds have such fine coats that they rarely need to be combed or brushed; simply stroking the cat's fur with

USA Champion Havana; the British type is finer boned with a wedge-shaped face

your hand is sufficient to remove any loose, dead hair. And the cat enjoys it too.

Havana
(see above)

The Havana is the chocolate-coloured version of the **Foreign** breed. The Havana was developed earlier than the other Foreigns, so was allowed to keep the name (from the name of the cigar) which the original breeders gave it. In every country but the United Kingdom, they are known as Orientals. They are striking-looking cats with chocolate coats and green eyes. Their looks reveal their **Siamese** ancestry, giving a clue to their character.

They are mischievous and playful, though softer-voiced than the Siamese. Havanas are highly intelligent cats, talkative and friendly towards their owners. They can be great extroverts, enjoying every opportunity to show off. People are very important to them and they may pine if separated from a loved owner. They will happily settle in a flat as it is people, not places, that are important to them. If living with a working owner, they need another cat of foreign type for company. Havanas love to have a cat friend with which to sleep curled up!

Havanas are robust due to early outcross-

79

ings and grooming is simple. Lively and happy-natured comedians, Havanas are cats of character.

haw

See **third eyelid**.

heartworm

See **worms**.

heating

Nature has already provided the domestic cat with a means of keeping warm by giving it a thick fur coat but there are times when extra heating is necessary. Newborn kittens, elderly cats and sick cats will all benefit from an additional source of heat, as will stud cats which live in outdoor runs, **Rex** cats which have very short coats, and **Sphynx** cats which are almost hairless.

Pet bed heaters are like small electric underblankets but are usually hard instead of soft, with the elements locked inside a metal base. They are inexpensive to run, using about a quarter of the power of a low power light bulb. They have been extensively used by breeders to keep warm newborn kittens, which can lose heat rapidly. However, a question mark may now hang over their use. Electromagnetic fields, such as those produced by electric blankets, are being implicated in a number of illnesses; some breeders have consequently gone back to using the old-fashioned hot water bottle.

Small space heaters (radiators) are specially made for areas such as stud houses by pet product manufacturers and are inexpensive to buy and run.

Cats are, of course, past masters at finding cosy places and will often end up in the airing cupboard or on top of a radiator or television set. This, however, should be discouraged in pregnant queens. There have been cases where queens have spent part of their pregnancy (in particular the early part) on top of a heat source, and have produced deformed kittens.

heat stroke

We may grumble at the British weather, but each year a distressingly high number of cats suffer heat stroke.

▷ symptoms: rapid breathing, drooling, red gums becoming blue. Later: coma, then death if not treated.

▷ treatment: provide good ventilation and fresh air. Immerse the cat up to the neck in cool water. Don't chill the cat – don't add ice cubes to the water, for example. If immersion is impossible, dampen cloths with cold water and cover the cat with them. As soon as the temperature is lowered, see your vet.

▷ prevention: don't leave cats in parked cars or other enclosed spaces exposed to direct sunlight.

hierarchy

There is a very definite hierarchy in any cat group, despite the myth of the solitary cat. At the top is the un-neutered tom – if there are several they will fight each other to become 'top cat'. Top cat gets certain privileges; he will be the first to eat so will get the best food and have his choice of the best sleeping area. He will also choose his own territory. He does not, however, have *carte blanche* with the females; females choose their own mates although, if a female lives in his territory, that must give him a big advantage.

Neutering and spaying alters the hierarchical structure; a neutered cat will always occupy a lower place in the hierarchy than an entire cat. A female's place is determined by the number of litters she has had so, in a home situation where all the cats are neutered, the dominant cat may be a female which has given birth to kittens.

Kittens occupy a special place on the hierarchical ladder. They will be deferred to over food by their own mother but not by unrelated cats. In fact, unrelated, entire toms may kill them when they are very young; this would result in their mother coming into season again more quickly, allowing the tom to mate with her. Once the kittens have survived the first, often dangerous, few weeks, they are tolerated well by other cats in the group. They do not become a threat until they are four to five months old, when they start to work their way up the hierarchical ladder. They will begin to challenge older cats by stealing their food or their sleeping places; sometimes they will get away with it without a fight, allowing them to move up another rung. At other times, the cat whose food or bed has been stolen will object and there might be a fight; if the kitten loses it knows not to bother that cat again – at least until it grows a little bigger.

Himalayan gene

The Himalayan gene colours and patterns the **Siamese** cat and its relatives, as well as the **Birman**, **Colourpoint Persian** and **Ragdoll**. In effect, it produces a cat with pale coloured body and darker coloured 'points' of which there are eight or nine – two ears, mask, four paws, tail and sexual organs (male only). Kittens coloured by the Himalayan gene are born white and their points colour develops as they mature. Cats coloured by the Himalayan gene continue to darken throughout their lives and their mask expands to cover their faces. Kittens are born with blue eyes – like all

other kittens – but they retain the blue eyes all their lives – unlike other cats.

The darker points occur on the cats' extremities, which would be expected to be colder than the rest of their body. Sunlight would then be absorbed by the dark fur, keeping the extremities warm, rather than be reflected by lighter fur.

Himalayan (also called the Malayan)

See **Colourpoint**.

holding

A cat or kitten should be held, firmly supported, with one hand under its bottom and the other hand around its back or chest. A cat will feel particularly secure if held in this way with the index finger of one hand between its two front paws and the middle finger and thumb on either side of the paws.

holidays

More and more people are taking their cats on holiday with them. Cats which are more people-oriented than territory-oriented (as are many of the pedigree breeds) will not be upset by a change of scene and may even enjoy it. Many hotels and caravan parks will allow animals to stay as long as they cause no damage, but you should make clear when booking that you will be bringing a pet.

A cat on holiday will need its litter tray and a supply of litter, its own food and water bowls and a supply of its favourite foods plus its carrier for travelling and a familiar blanket to sleep on. It should wear a collar with its addresses on it – its holiday address and its home address. Most holidaying cats are indoor cats and and should not, of course, be allowed out of doors on holiday except on a leash. See also **catteries**.

homing

Cats have 'homed' over remarkable distances and it still is not known how they do it. Some people believe that they are sensitive to the earth's magnetic field, possessing natural, built-in compasses. This would explain results of experiments such as the one where a cat was rowed into the middle of a lake. Whichever way the boat was turned, and whether the cat was able to see or not, it always climbed to the part of the boat nearest home. However, sensitivity to magnetic fields would not explain those cases where a cat has walked long distances, not back to its previous home, but to a new home it had never seen and where the owners had settled without it. A cat called Sugar walked from his home in California, where he had been left with a neighbour, to his owners' new farm in Oklahoma, a distance of 1,500 miles. It took him 13 months.

homoeopathy

Homoeopathy, treating an illness with diluted and minute amounts of substances which, in larger quantities, are capable of reproducing the symptoms of the illness, can be used on animals. Some vets practise homoeopathy alongside their conventional veterinary skills. Amongst other remedies, homoeopathic practitioners claim oral vaccines against **feline leukaemia virus**, **feline infectious peritonitis** and **feline infectious anaemia**. Several books have been written on homoeopathic first aid for pets and homoeopathic pet remedies.

hookworms

See **worms**.

hot

When a cream-coloured cat has a red tinge to its coat, it is referred to as being hot. Red cats have their hair pigment dispersed in a regular manner; cream cats have the pigment dispersed in an irregular manner, creating the optical illusion of the paler colour. Sometimes the 'true' red colour shows through on the cream coat – much to the chagrin of the cat's breeder.

housebound cats

See **indoor cats**.

household pet

Another name for the non-pedigree cat, particularly at cat shows which hold sections for competitors which are not purebred.

houseplants

See **poisonous plants**.

hunting

Training for hunting starts around four weeks of age. A mother cat will wave her tail from side to side and her kittens, attracted by the movement, will pounce on it, using the same pouncing technique they will later use on their prey. Movement attracts a cat and triggers the hunting instinct; they have specific brain cells which respond to movement.

For the next lesson in hunting a mother cat will bring back small, dead prey animals for her kittens to practise on. They will toss the dead animals about in a form of play which teaches them about the feel and smell of prey. Next, a live prey animal will be brought back to the nest for the kittens to catch and kill.

Kittens which do not have this early training may never be very good at catching prey but they will still possess the hunting instinct; even cats which come from long lines of indoor cats will chase and catch insects in the home. Insects would, in fact, form part of a feral cat's diet, as would mice, rats, birds, rabbits and even occasionally fish, depending on a cat's territory.

The behaviour which upsets so many animal lovers, when a cat catches its prey and lets it go, only to catch it again, is due to the cat's hunting instinct being triggered by movement. It will catch a prey animal which, if it 'plays dead' is left alone, only to be caught again when it begins to move. For the same reason, a cat will catch prey even when it is not hungry and does not eat what it has caught. Living wild, a cat would hide any food not immediately wanted by scratching leaves on top to cover it. You may sometimes see your own pet scratching around its food bowl to 'hide' the contents, either because it is not very hungry or because the food is not particularly palatable.

Tossing its prey about and hitting it on the head is also seen as cruelty. However, a cat could receive a serious bite from a rodent, the wound could become infected and ultimately kill it. For its own safety, a cat will toss its prey about to disorient and stun it. It will also hit its prey on the head. This will make it lower its head, which prevents it from biting the cat and also presents the neck in the right position for the cat to give a killing bite if it is able to get in close enough. The cat will kill by a single bite, severing the spinal cord and it has even been suggested that cats have varying distances between their long canine teeth which are purpose-built for killing different types of prey.

If cats are kept as mousers, they should be well cared for and well fed. Properly fed cats make better mousers, while those kept hungry can lack the energy for the chase. If you wish to try to discourage your cat from hunting see **birds**.

hyperthyroidism

Hyperthyroidism is a 'new' disease of the old cat. First noticed around 1979, it is not uncommon in cats from middle age onwards. The earliest age at which a cat is known to have been affected is 6 years and the mean age is around 11½ years.

▷ symptoms: voracious appetite yet loss of weight, fast heart rate, increased activity, restlessness, nervousness, intolerance of heat, aggression, an anxious facial expression.
▷ cause: not known
▷ treatment: the cat's thyroid gland may be removed, although some cats have become hyperthyroid again after its removal due to the action of the thyroid tissue in the chest. An antithyroid drug may be given, or radiation treatment.

I

inbreeding

If closely related cats are mated to each other, it is referred to as inbreeding. Many consider this practice critically saying, quite correctly, that the more genes the parents have in common, the more likely they are to pass on any faults they possess to their offspring. However, it is also true that if the parents are healthy, beautiful cats, they are as likely to pass *these* qualities on. Inbreeding should only be undertaken by very experienced breeders with a sound knowledge of genetics and an understanding of their cats' pedigrees.

incontinence

See **soiling**.

Independent Pet Cat Society

A British organisation which holds cat shows for non-pedigree cats and pet quality pedigree cats with the blessing of the **GCCF**.

indoor cats

More and more cats of all types are being kept completely indoors and never allowed out to roam. Is this cruel? If you consider the fact that half of all cats are killed in road accidents and that the lifespan of the average indoor cat is about twice that of the average outdoor cat, the answer has to be no – as long as you provide your indoor cat with all it needs.

Chief among the indoor cat's requirements is companionship. It is unable to go out of doors to find its own companions, so relies on you to do so. Companionship can be human, or feline, just as long as the indoor cat is not left alone all day to become bored and unhappy – because it will.

If you can set aside some time each day to **play** with your indoor cat, especially if it is an 'only' cat, this will benefit its health and its sense of well-being, just as an aerobics workout benefits a human.

Make sure the indoor cat has a comfortable place to sleep, a private toilet area and a type of litter it likes to use. Some cats prefer one type of litter to another and the indoor cat has no choice; it must use what you provide. It also needs some greenery as an aid to digestion, places to climb and hide, and something it is allowed to strop its claws on. See the separate headings: **beds**, **climbers**, **grass**, **litter (2)**, **play** and **scratching furniture**.

An indoor cat may need a vitamin supplement if its fur becomes dull and lifeless or its skin scaly, or if it becomes listless and uninterested in its food or surroundings. An indoor cat may become deficient in vitamin D, for example. An outdoor cat synthesises the vitamin on its coat from sunlight, which an indoor cat is unable to do, living in a sunny home, as ultra violet cannot penetrate glass.

Ideally, an indoor cat should have a safe

wire mesh run in the garden, or a wire mesh screen to fit over an open window, so it can sunbathe in safety.

Although many cats will adapt happily to flat or apartment life, it is important that the home is spacious enough to allow the cat to play, hide and have a change of scenery. It isn't fair to expect a cat, particularly an **indoor cat**, to live in a small, one-roomed apartment.

influenza

See **Feline Respiratory Disease**.

inoculations (injections)

In the United Kingdom, only one annual injection is currently given to cats, this is the combined vaccination for enteritis and cat 'flu (**feline infectious enteritis** and **feline respiratory disease**). A kitten is protected from these illnesses for the first two months of life by antibodies from its mother's milk but then needs an inoculation, given at about nine weeks of age. A second inoculation is given three to four weeks later and then boosters are given annually. A kitten is not fully protected until about a week after the second injection and should be kept indoors until then.

Rabies is endemic in most parts of the world and rabies vaccinations are started at three months of age, after which annual boosters are given. Only the UK, Australia, New Zealand, Hawaii and Scandinavia (except Fin-

Introductions require tact, but there will still be spitting and fighting (page 86)

land) are free from rabies at the time of writing.

Feline Leukaemia Virus (FeLV) is another killer of cats for which vaccinations are available in the USA and many European countries but not in the UK. Vaccinations are given at around nine weeks of age, followed by a second vaccination three weeks later, with a third two months after the second; thereafter annual boosters are given. At the time of writing, this vaccine has not been accepted by UK veterinary bodies because of the risk of side effects and the fact that only 65% of cats vaccinated develop immunity.

Preventive injections should be budgeted for when working out the cost of keeping a cat; although they add a little to the yearly budget, they can save a lot of money in veterinary fees in the long run.

insurance

There's no National Health Service for cats and veterinary bills nowadays can be high as treatments become ever more sophisticated and expensive. Pet health insurance can take the worry out of veterinary bills. If your cat becomes ill, an insurance company will pay for the veterinary treatment. Different health insurance schemes vary in the cover they provide and prices vary too, so several schemes should be compared before you decide which one to choose.

For a yearly or quarterly premium, you can insure your cat for each course of veterinary treatment (excluding the first few pounds which you will have to pay) and for third party insurance to cover legal liability for injury or damage caused by your pet (more important for dog owners than cat owners). Some schemes will also pay replacement costs if your cat is killed accidentally, lost or stolen, and may even pay advertising costs and/or a

reward. Some will also pay the cost of cattery fees if the owner has to spend time in hospital.

Preventive treatment such as special diets or inoculations are not covered by insurance, neither is the cost of neutering or spaying, or, usually, costs for treatment for kittening. There is at least one insurance company with a special policy for breeders which *will* cover the cost of kittening treatment so it is important to shop around to ensure you have the cover you need.

Some of the companies will pay your vet direct while others will expect you to pay the bills yourself and reclaim the money from them. This could be an important point to bear in mind when choosing a policy as bills can easily rise to hundreds of pounds for a continuing course of treatment or to repair the damage of an accident.

Don't wait until your cat gets old before insuring it; insurance companies will not accept cats over eight or ten years of age. If your cat is under that age, check that the company's policy is to continue insurance cover for the elderly cat.

intestinal worms

See **worms**.

intermediate certificates

See **recognition**.

introductions   (see page 85)

A great deal of care and patience should be used when introducing a kitten or cat into a household where there is already a cat. The existing cat is not going to be happy to see the newcomer, even if you are convinced it needs a companion. The newcomer will be seen as a threat, so it is up to you to make the introductions as unthreatening and painless as possible.

First, quarantine the newcomer for several days, if possible. Keep it in a separate room with a separate litter tray and separate feeding bowls. It may be harbouring some infection which could take several days to show up; a quarantine period should ensure that it is healthy when you finally introduce it to your existing cat (see **quarantine of a new cat or kitten**).

It is vital that you allow your cat to make friends with the newcomer before it sees *you* making friends with it. So have your cat on your lap when the newcomer is brought into the room. (If possible, have a friend bring the newcomer in; then it will be associated in your cat's mind with your friend, not you.)

Your cat will jump down to inspect the newcomer; allow it to do so and don't interfere. A great deal of hissing, spitting and feline argument will follow as it is essential for the cats to work out who is to be boss. If the newcomer is a kitten, despite its youth it will be an expert on body language, making itself appear small and insignificant when confronted by an assertive cat and looking big and bouncing if confronted by a timid cat.

Kittens will fit into a household within a day or two, if left to their own devices. If the newcomer is an adult cat, it will take much longer to become accepted and to accept your other cat(s). Fighting may produce blood-curdling noises but you should not break them up unless one of the cats is actually being hurt, which is fairly unlikely. Most owners give up too quickly; they fear the cats are being hurt and separate them, which just makes the introductory period take much longer. Only separate the cats for the first few nights if you are really concerned about them and at other times when you are not around to supervise.

Ensure there are a few places around the room where the newcomer can hide if the argument becomes too much for it to handle. Empty cardboard boxes are ideal. And trim the cats' claws – they are less likely to hurt one another with blunt claws.

Make sure both felines have separate beds and separate feeding bowls. Expecting a cat to share its food with a stranger is a recipe for disaster. If you want to call a break to the spitting and hissing, feeding the cats may take their minds off each other. Feed both at the same time but place the feeding bowls at least six feet apart. Cats dislike eating close to strangers. The bowls can be placed closer together as they gradually become used to one another.

J

Jacobson's organ

This organ, unique to the cat family, combines taste and smell. When using it, a cat will show the **flehmen response**, tasting and smelling the air at the same time. The lips will roll back allowing air to pass over the roof of the mouth and the cat will appear to grimace. It is used when danger threatens, to test the air; when a cat is anxious and by the tomcat in response to a queen in oestrus.

Because the senses of smell and taste are so closely linked in the cat, a sick cat may not eat if it is unable to smell its food. It should be fed strong smelling food such as pilchards, tuna or sardines.

Japanese Bobtail   *(see opposite)*

Bobtails are the ancient cat of Japan and are very striking in looks. Their tails are short with a 'bob' on the end and sometimes look like a rabbit's tail. Unlike the **Manx**, two Bobtails will always produce short-tailed offspring, while a Bobtail mated with any other type of cat will always produce offspring with normal-length tails.

Japanese Bobtails are known for their outgoing personalities. They are friendly towards one another and to their owners, wagging their short tails in greeting and to show pleasure. They are talkative and agile cats, enjoying climbing and chasing after small toys, which they will retrieve. They are known as highly-intelligent cats, yet with gentle, attractive personalities.

In colour, they are usually white with bold black or red markings. Some have both black and red markings on their white background which looks very beautiful and is considered extremely lucky in the Far East. This is called the Mi-Ke pattern although many other colours are now being bred.

The Bobtails' soft coats are easy to groom and a once-weekly combing will keep them looking their best.

jealousy

Many owners don't realise that jealousy can be an all-consuming passion with their cats. Cats are renowned for their independence, yet they become very attached to their owners, transferring all the feelings they had for their mothers to their new, human 'mums'. So they can become jealous of other cats in the household – or even of their owner's spouse.

Jealousy will lead to fighting, hissing, growling and other anti-social behaviour, but can be minimised if the cats have been properly introduced. This is vital as the behaviour pattern between cats can be set

Unlike the Manx, two Japanese Bobtails always produce bobtailed kittens

at the first meeting. See **introductions**.

Cats can become jealous of new members of the household, such as a baby. Jealousy won't lead to any violent behaviour, however. A cat is much more likely to show that it is feeling left out of things by urinating on its owner's bed or on a carpet. All you can do if this happens is to try to make more of a fuss of your cat and spend more time with it. Chas-

tisement will make the problem worse. See **soiling**.

jowls

Older cats, usually male and usually entire, often have jowls – well-developed cheeks. Early neutering prevents the development of jowls, giving a neutered male a more 'feminine' appearance.

K

Karthusian

See **Chartreuse**.

Key-Gaskell syndrome

See **Feline Dysautonomia**.

kidneys

The kidneys filter waste products from the blood, expelling toxic substances as urine. If this filtering function becomes less effective, the toxic substances remain in the body, and the cat becomes ill.

Kidney disease, in which kidney tissue is destroyed, occurs frequently in the older cat. Symptoms are increased thirst and increased volume of urine, as well as loss of weight. Veterinary advice should be sought immediately and will probably include a change of diet to one containing less protein and more carbohydrate. Vitamin supplements and drugs may also be prescribed. In more advanced cases of kidney disease there will be vomiting, bad breath, anaemia, dehydration and possibly convulsions.

Nephritis (inflammation of the kidneys) can have a number of causes, and symptoms are increased thirst with loss of weight. Appetite will be poor and the cat will appear dejected. There may be a 'pot belly' due to an accumulation of fluid in the abdomen.

kink

Legend has it that the kink in the tail of the **Siamese** appeared after a Siamese princess, bathing in a river, was looking for somewhere safe to place her precious rings. Her Siamese cat obligingly crooked its tail so that she could place the rings on its tail without them falling off again.

Charming though this legend is, it glosses over the fact that a kinked tail is an inherited deformity in some breeds caused by a malformation of the vertebrae and is now considered a disqualifying fault in a show cat. Some cats, born with perfect tails, acquire a kink in later life, usually as a result of their tails being caught in a door or some other accident.

kitten

A young cat aged up to nine months in the United Kingdom. After nine months, it is regarded as an adult cat. In the USA, a kitten is not regarded as adult until ten months of age.

kittening

The first sign that birth is imminent may be when the female looks for a nest site. If one has already been provided, she may go into it. She may become agitated and unable to settle and may even wake her owners, if it is night.

It is very important to most cats to have human company while giving birth, although a few will prefer to deal with the entire process on their own.

Ensure that a suitable kittening box is provided several days before the birth is due. This can be a large cardboard box, which has contained a 'clean', non-smelling product, such as potato crisps. A similar box with a hole cut in the side can be placed over the top of this to simulate a secure dark nest. Line the kittening box with several layers of newspaper, for warmth, and cover this with sheets of kitchen towel paper, which can be replaced as necessary.

Have ready the following equipment:

▷ sterilised, round-ended scissors
▷ thread
▷ a clean towel
▷ a tin of milk substitute, formulated for kittens, in case the mother is unable to feed them
▷ a medicine dropper or small animal feeding bottle

Make sure that the room in which the kittening is taking place is very warm, quiet and free from all disturbance.

When birth is imminent, your cat may begin to pant or purr and there may be a clear discharge from the vulva, or a spot of blood. This stage can last several hours, but is usually much shorter than that, especially in cats which have kittened before.

Contractions will start and continue for ten to thirty minutes. If they last longer than ninety minutes without producing a kitten, telephone your vet. When the first kitten is born, the mother may deal with it, or she may leave it to you. Equally, she may deal with the first kitten but leave the remaining ones to your care, as she feeds her first kitten. If she is

happily carrying out the following functions, allow her to do so, otherwise you must do it yourself.

If the mother has not dealt with the kittens, gently grasp the skin of the birth sac, tearing it open. It is very fragile and requires little effort to open. Leaving the umbilical cord intact for the moment, make sure the kitten's nose is clear and it is breathing. Then rub the kitten dry with the towel.

Tie a piece of thread several inches from the kitten's abdomen and cut the cord on the placenta (afterbirth) side, using sterilised scissors. The end of the cord can be dabbed with a special antiseptic solution which can be obtained from your vet. This will prevent any infection of the umbilical cord. Place the kitten at its mother's teats and watch to see that it begins to suck. A lusty kitten will suckle immediately, even if its mother's milk is scanty at first. Its sucking will help stimulate the milk flow. The first milk, or colostrum, is particularly important to a kitten as it contains antibodies vital to keep a kitten in good health during its first few weeks.

Count the placentas as they are expelled to make sure that there is one for every kitten. If not, you must consult your vet as a retained placenta will set up an infection. The placentas may appear almost immediately as the kittens are born or take half an hour or more; don't pull, allow them to appear in their own time. The queen may want to eat the placentas and should be allowed to eat one or two if she wishes; it is believed they have a function in starting milk to flow. She will be relieved if you dispose of the rest for her; several can cause a tummy upset, and she is simply trying to keep her nest clean.

The kittens must be kept warm and their mother will usually curl around them to ensure this. If one becomes cold and sluggish,

91

The yellowish eyes of this female Korat show
she is not yet mature

you should immerse it up to the neck in hand-warm water.

If a kitten is having difficulty breathing, ensure its nose and mouth have been cleaned of mucus, hold it at arm's length in the palm of your hand and swing your arm downward, stopping abruptly with the kitten's nose pointing towards the floor. Repeat this several times until breathing is restored and the kitten begins to cry and wriggle.

Call your vet if:

▷ your cat seems uneasy or distressed
▷ she strains for more than an hour without success
▷ there is more than three hours between kittens
▷ she passes a yellow or green discharge, or blood, before the kittens are born
▷ there is blood or any other discharge after the kittens are born
▷ your cat appears to be going into labour early (before nine weeks).

Cats usually make very good mothers but if for some reason your cat is unable to feed her kittens, you will have to feed them using a milk substitute available from pet stores and vets. Don't give them cow's milk, except as an emergency measure, as it does not contain enough protein. Feed them at two-hourly intervals, using a medical dropper or small animal feeding bottle. Their tummies should be gently rubbed and their bottoms wiped after each meal until they eliminate waste; they cannot do this for themselves for four weeks.

Keep visitors away from any kittens for the first few weeks and only let visitors handle older kittens if they have washed their hands thoroughly first. Infection can be passed on very easily to young kittens.

kneading

When kittens are suckling their mother they will knead on either side of her teats with their paws. This helps the milk flow. Kneading then becomes associated in a cat's mind with a pleasurable experience – being fed – and in later life a cat will knead every time it is feeling happy. Most cats will knead their owners' laps prior to settling down, as their owners have become surrogate 'mums'. Although this can be painful, it is unlikely that an owner will be able to persuade their cat to stop kneading and it would probably be unkind to try. Trimming the cat's claws and wearing thick trousers are the only remedies.

Korat   (see opposite)

Korats originated in Thailand, where they are considered lucky cats, but they are still uncommon, even in their home country.

They have beautiful silver-blue fur and remarkable green-gold eyes with a penetrating gaze. Kittens may not develop the green eyes for a year or two; at first they are yellow.

Sweet-natured and loving, they like to play, even well past kittenhood, and are always ready for a romp or game. They are sociable cats, loving human companionship and are full of fun. They make good family pets and do not mind sharing a home with a dog, as long as **introductions** are properly carried out. They make good pets for the town and flat dweller as they do not want to go far from home, especially female Korats. They will happily stay indoors as they dislike extremes of temperature. They like company, as do most cats, and should not be left alone. Another Korat or foreign-type cat would make good company.

Grooming is simple and Korats enjoy a healthy, mixed diet.

L

labour

See **kittening**.

lactational tetany

See **eclampsia**.

leash-training

If you have never seen a cat walking on a leash you may be surprised to learn how easy it is to train a cat to do so – although you may have to walk where your cat wants to rather than where *you* want to. More and more cats are being trained to walk on a leash as the safest way of exercising. Some of the pedigree breeds take readily to leash training, in particular the **Siamese**, **Foreigns**, and **Rex**, but virtually any cat can be leash-trained, if this is done in the proper manner. It is easier to train a young cat than an old cat, but, with patience, it *is* possible to teach an old cat new tricks. Don't expect to put a harness and leash on your cat on the first day; it can take weeks to get to that stage.

First, accustom your cat to wearing a collar. The collar should be placed around its neck for the training period only; a few minutes at first, then ten, then half an hour. Stay with your cat while it is wearing the collar and, after the training period is over, remove the collar for safety's sake. If your cat has never worn a collar before, buy some of its favourite treats, give it one and, while it is enjoying eating it, slip the collar round its neck. Fasten the collar so that you can place one finger between the collar and your cat's neck. Tighter than that, it is too tight; looser than that and your cat will catch its paw or lower jaw in the collar in an attempt to get it off. More treats can be given to take its mind off wearing the collar but don't overdo it; the idea is to exercise your cat, not make it hopelessly fat.

Continue this every day, for a longer period each time, until your cat is perfectly at ease while wearing the collar. However, a collar is not a suitable restraint for a cat on a leash; most cats are very good at slipping out of it. The collar is simply to get your cat used to wearing something around its neck. An 'H' shaped harness should be used for complete safety. This buckles around the neck and chest and is much safer than the cheaper type of harness, consisting of two loops with an adjustable fastener which slides along the loops.

Remove your cat's collar and fasten the harness in position, giving treats to take your cat's mind off the new restraint. Leave the harness on for a few minutes, increasing the time day by day. When your cat is happy with the harness, attach the leash, holding it loosely. Stand as far away from your cat as you can while still holding the leash, calling your cat to you and rewarding it with a treat when it responds. You can then start walking slowly, calling the cat along with you and rewarding it with a treat from time to time. Keep the weight of the leash off your cat's back, at least at first, as many cats find this off-putting.

leukaemia

See **Feline Leukaemia Virus (FeLV)**.

lice

If a cat is run down or ill and stops grooming, lice may take advantage of the situation and hop aboard. These tiny greyish insects, the size of a pinhead, will bite a cat or suck its blood, causing it to become even more run down and anaemic. Lice are not easy to see but their white eggs, attached to individual hairs, may be seen. Most flea treatments are effective against lice too but will have to be given in a course of three treatments at ten-day intervals. This is because the insecticide will kill the lice but not the eggs, which will continue to hatch.

If the lice problem is severe and the cat has broken skin, do not use any flea treatment or insecticide on the cat but seek veterinary advice. Treatment should also be given for the initial problem which caused the cat to become run down or ill.

Lice found on a cat will not live on humans and vice versa.

lifespan

The average lifespan of a cat is considered to be around 14 to 15 years of age for males; a year or two more for females. Like humans, a cat with long-lived parents will live longer too, barring accidents. Research has shown that neutered cats live longer than entire cats and that indoor cats live longest of all, on average twice as long as indoor/outdoor cats. Feral cats can expect a lifespan of just six years. The oldest cat whose age could be verified was a tabby from Devon which lived to 34 years 5 months.

lifting

Never lift a cat or kitten by the scruff of the neck as it puts an undue strain on their neck muscles. A mother cat lifts her kittens that way but she doesn't have hands! Support your cat with one hand under its bottom and the other around its chest or back.

lilac

Lilac, although quite rare, is sometimes seen as a coat colour. It is a pinkish-blue hue. **Burmese** and **Persian** are bred in a lilac version. The **Siamese** can have lilac-coloured points.

line-breeding

A cat may be mated with a close relative, for example, a grandson or grandfather, to try to pass on any particularly good points they possess. See also **inbreeding**.

lip licking

Lip licking is a nervous reaction in a cat and it will be seen to do this when feeling uneasy – which is why cats are often licking their lips in photographs!

liquid paraffin

Liquid paraffin is a clear, oily liquid which can be purchased from a chemist and should not be confused with the fuel which burns in paraffin stoves and lamps. Liquid paraffin, also called medicinal liquid paraffin, is useful when a cat is suffering from a **hairball**. Giving the cat one 5ml teaspoon of liquid paraffin a day for a maximum of three or four days should dislodge it. Liquid paraffin should not be given to a cat for a period longer than four days as it coats the lining of stomach and intestines, affecting the absorption of nutrients from the cat's food.

litter (1)

A litter is the name given to a group of kittens all born to the same mother at about the same time. In fact, some cats will give birth to a kitten and not produce another one for perhaps 24 hours. Both kittens are, nevertheless, from the same litter. An average litter size is around two or three kittens for a first litter, and around four kittens in subsequent litters. Average litter size varies according to the breed of cat. The largest litter ever recorded was one of 19 kittens, four of which were stillborn, to a Burmese from Oxfordshire.

litter (2)

Litter is also the name given to the filler in a cat's litter box or tray. It was 'invented' in the USA in 1947, by a man who sold industrial absorbents. Before that date, cats had had to make do with earth, cinders or newspaper.

The most popular types are the clay litters. These are natural clays, dug out of the earth, crushed, dried and bagged, usually with nothing added.

Fullers' Earth is a heavy grey clay; its technical name is *calcium montomorillonite*. It is extremely absorbent, holding moisture up to 125% of its own weight. It is an inexpensive litter and is excellent at absorbing smells. It works best when the tray is filled to a depth of several inches; liquid waste then forms a ball which is easily lifted out leaving the clean, dry clay behind.

Two other clay litters, *attapulgite* and *sepiolite*, are white and absorb moisture up to 110% of their own weight. *Moeler clay*, another type of litter, is pinkish in colour; it is not very widely available in the United Kingdom.

A few manufacturers add deodorants to their litter and some owners add litter deodorant themselves. This is usually more popular among owners than cats who will sometimes stop using treated litter and may even show an allergic reaction to it.

A growing proportion of the cat litter market is being taken over by wood-based litters. These are basically softwoods which have been turned into sawdust and pelletised. They are extremely absorbent, absorbing up to 300% of their own volume, and usually turning back to sawdust in the process. Their natural odour-absorbing properties are good as far as liquid waste is concerned but poor when dealing with faeces. Wood litters should be used in shallow depths as they expand when wet.

A new type of cat litter is made from pelletised corncobs coated with food-grade paraffin wax. This litter is totally washable and reusable. Liquid waste filters through the litter, through the slotted tray in which it is contained, and into another tray underneath, from which it can be drained away. This type of litter, excellent for liquid waste, has no deodorising properties for solid waste. It is very useful when a urine sample is required, as the sample can be collected from the tray at the bottom without difficulty.

Alternatives to manufactured litters are available. Litter trays can be filled with shredded newspaper (which can afterwards be burnt), peat or earth (which can be put on the compost heap) or smooth gravel or pebbles (which can be drained and washed).

litter trays

Litter trays vary from the basic, inexpensive plastic tray to purpose-built trays for reusable litter (see above). The basic plastic tray is fine for most cats, but scattering the litter can be a problem. If so, the tray can be placed in a cardboard box, or a box can be upended over it, with a door cut in the side. This not only cuts down on scatter, but gives the cat privacy – and most cats like privacy. Manufacturers realise this and have produced a version of the plastic tray with a covered top, which cats enjoy using.

Some kittens, used to covered litter trays and confronted by an open or 'public' tray in their new home, cross their legs and won't use it. Most cats will also prefer a tray which is carefully sited – in a quiet, out of the way spot, where there is not a lot of passing traffic to disturb them.

liver

See **offal**.

loneliness

For a very long time the cat has been characterised as a solitary, independent creature. Yet this is hardly borne out by the facts. Cats live, for choice, in groups. Whether those groups be feline or human, they expect companionship and affection. Without these, they become withdrawn and unhappy; even destructive.

Yet many owners still acquire a cat because they think they can be left alone all day, with no ill effects. This is not the case at all. A cat no more enjoys a solitary existence than we do. If you have a cat, and have to go out to work, make sure your cat has company, feline or human. It will be much happier and boredom-related destructiveness should not occur.

longhair

Longhair describes the cat which many owners call 'fluffy'. It has also been used to describe the **Persian**, the pedigree breed with very long fur. Longhairs seem to have sprung up at around the same time (16th century) in remote, mountainous areas of the world such as Persia, Turkey and China, where their long fur would have served an important purpose in keeping them warm.

lungworms

See **worms**.

lynx-point

Name in the USA for tabby-point. Has also been called the silver-point.

M

mackerel

One of the patterns seen in the tabby coat. Mackerel tabbies are those with numerous small markings, closely set together, reminiscent of the fish after which the pattern is named.

mad moments

Every cat has them – those 'mad' moments when it will rush around the house like a wild thing, scattering everything in its wake. It often puzzles an owner that their cat can be sleeping peacefully one moment and ricocheting around the house the next. However, to the cat it is just a way of getting rid of surplus energy.

When it has nothing to do, a cat will conserve energy by sleeping for long periods. That 'stored-up' energy will be unleashed in a quick burst when the cat has to hunt for food. Our domestic cats no longer need to hunt but they still have that energy to expend. You can help your cat use up its excessive energy by a regular exercise period each evening (see **play**).

Maine Coon   (see opposite)

Although the breed developed in the USA, its origins are mysterious. Some believe these cats were brought to America by Vikings in the 11th century while others think they were the pets of the New England settlers. The Maine Coon's big, fluffy tail accounts for the 'Coon' part of the name. At one time, it was believed (wrongly) that they were descended from a cross between a cat and a wild racoon, which has a thick tail and is called a coon for short.

The Maine Coon's coat is silky yet shaggy and rarely mats. They have furry breeches and fanned-out tails as long as their bodies. Their feet are wide, natural 'snowshoes'. They are strong, heavy cats; the adult male weighs between 15 to 20lb (6.8 to 9.07kg) and the female 7 to 12lb (3.5 to 5.5kg). They do not attain their full size until they are three or four years old, as they are slow to mature and will remain kittenish for several years.

Maine Coons are extremely sociable and become devoted to their owners. They are very playful, yet highly intelligent and independent. The hardiness of the Maine Coon is a byword. They are extremely adaptable cats and love to run free, playing happily with feline and human friends.

They are bred in many colours, including white, tabby and tortoiseshell. Grooming is not difficult because of the silkiness of their coats.

Although the Maine Coon was the first show cat in the USA, they later went through a period of unpopularity during which numbers dwindled. Later still, however, they became so sought-after that there were reports

Blotched Blue Tabby female Maine Coon

of 'counterfeit' Maine Coons, using crosses between longhairs and non-pedigree cats! They have become increasingly popular in the United Kingdom since their introduction in the mid 1980s.

Maltese

Until the beginning of the 20th century, any shorthaired blue cat was referred to as a Maltese cat in the United Kingdom. However, the term is not an accurate name for any breed of cat and is never used by anyone knowledgeable about cats.

Mandarin

See **Angora**.

mange

Mange is the name given to a skin condition caused by infestation with parasitic mites. There are several different mites that cause mange in cats and the signs vary depending on which mite is involved. Diagnosis is usually made by a skin scraping to identify the mite involved using a microscope and also by the characteristic signs associated with the different mites. Treatment can include spraying with an anti-parasitic product or tablets. Care must be taken to follow instructions carefully.

Manx   (see pages 102 and 103)

There are several legends about the arrival of the tailless Manx on the Isle of Man. It is thought some may have swum ashore from a shipwrecked galleon of the Spanish Armada, or that they may have been brought to the island from Japan, where there is a short-tailed indigenous cat called the Bobtail. One charming legend accounting for the Manx's taillessness tells of cats which played while storms raged in Biblical times, ignoring

Noah's call to the safety of the Ark. Finally, the Ark was ready to set sail – and the quick cats were able to slip inside just as the doors closed. But the doors closed on their tails, chopping them off and creating a breed of cat which would be forever tailless.

As so often happens, reality is much more mundane. Their taillessness (or shortened tail) is a result of a semi-lethal gene which causes abnormalities in the vertebrae and leads to some Manx kittens dying in the womb. For this reason, some people believe that the breed should not be perpetuated, although in every Manx to Manx mating one-third of the kittens will have normal tails.

Theoretically tailless, many Manx do, in fact, have tails of a sort. 'Rumpy' is the name given to a completely tailless cat, a 'rumpy riser' has a tiny tail at the end of a shortened spine, a 'stumpy' has a definite tiny tail which is the extension of the spinal bones and 'longies' have short to normal-length tails.

Manx cats, whatever their tails are like, look larger than they are due to their rounded backs and thick, double coats, which can be of any colour. Their hind legs are longer than the front, giving them their characteristic hopping gait.

The word most often used to describe the Manx's personality is 'dog-like'. They are dog-like in their devotion to their owners and are often friendly with dogs. In fact, in the last century, one Manx cat was often exhibited with a bulldog. Manx cats are faithful and intelligent companions, providing company and amusement for their owners.

There is a longhaired version of the Manx called the Cymric (see page 103).

marbled

More commonly known as classic, marbled describes the basic tabby pattern.

mask

Cats with coats patterned by the **Himalayan gene** have light-coloured bodies with dark points. The face over the eyes and nose is dark in colour and this, for obvious reasons, is referred to as a mask.

massage

You probably enjoy stroking your cat. After all, the beneficial effects on humans are well known – lowered blood pressure and a decrease in stress. Undoubtedly your cat enjoys being stroked. Massaging your cat is an extension of stroking, and it helps relieve the effects of some feline ailments such as **cystitis**, **kidney** problems and arthritis.

Don't use oil when massaging a cat and always stroke in the direction of the fur, and don't touch either the backbone or windpipe.

Place your cat on your lap and slowly stroke it from head to tail until it begins to relax. Then with the flat part of your fingertips gently massage along its sides from neck to tail using small circular movements. Still using circular movements, massage the back of the neck and stroke the front of the neck (but not the windpipe) with vertical movements. Then, one at a time, gently massage the legs in a downward motion and massage between each paw pad, jiggling each toe. Finish by using circular movements on the abdomen and then gently stroke all over.

mastitis

If a nursing queen refuses to feed her kittens, it may be due to an infection or inflammation of her teats, which will cause her pain. If there is an abnormal secretion from the teats, or the queen has a temperature, or the kittens have diarrhoea or the queen's 'breasts' appear hot or swollen, mastitis should be suspected and veterinary attention sought immediately.

Antibiotics may be prescribed and owners can make their cats feel more comfortable by bathing the affected teat or teats with a warm **salt-water solution**.

mating

Female cats, unlike human females, ovulate in response to mating. Cats, left to their own devices, will almost always mate successfully. A male cat will be attracted by the scent of a queen in heat over a very long distance and will pursue her avidly. In the pedigree world, where matings are arranged, a calling queen will be taken to a stud cat for mating. Breeders will try to choose a stud which lives nearby and hope that the weather will not turn too cold – a long journey or a change in the weather may lead to a queen going off call if she becomes stressed or uncomfortable. A pedigree queen, being mated for the first time, should be introduced to her beau gradually. She should be placed in a pen where she is able to see and smell the stud cat, but where they are kept separate at first.

When they are put together, the two cats will sniff and lick one another and the male may spray over the female, then, when the queen is ready, she will crouch down with her pelvis raised and her tail held to one side. The male will mount her, gripping the skin at the back of her neck so that she will stay still. When he dismounts after ejaculating, the queen may scream and slash at him with claws and teeth. It is thought that the barbed tip of the male's penis may cause the queen pain on withdrawal.

The mating of pedigree cats is usually supervised by the stud owner to ensure that mating takes place and also to make sure that the cats do not hurt each other. Some cats just seem to be incompatible and will not mate; instead they can end up having a violent fight.

Mau

See **Oriental Tabby** and **Spotted**.

medicine (giving)

See **pills (giving)**. To give a liquid medicine, hold your cat's head as described for giving pills, having wrapped the cat in a towel first if it threatens to object. It is much easier to give medicine from a dropper than a teaspoon and these can be purchased from chemists for a few pence. Place the dropper (or spoon) at the side of your cat's mouth, behind the large canine tooth. There is a gap in the teeth here and the medicine will go into the mouth without difficulty. Give a few drops at a time or your cat may choke with the medicine going into the lungs and causing damage. If in doubt about administering medicines, ask your vet for a demonstration when the medicine is prescribed.

memory

As any cat lover knows, felines have excellent memories. There are many instances of cats remembering and greeting humans they have met only once, several years earlier. Experiments carried out at the universities of Princeton and Pennsylvania involved cats being rewarded with food when they pressed a number of plates in a predetermined order. Cats, and even kittens, were able to remember sequences of up to seven presses and help themselves to food.

At the University of Michigan, food was hidden in a box surrounded by numerous other boxes. A light was briefly lit above the box containing the food and the cats were prevented from approaching any of the boxes so that it could be determined how long they could remember which box had been lit. Cats were able to remember this information for up to sixteen hours, while dogs could only

Brown Tabby female Manx (page 99)

remember where the food was for five minutes!

milk

See **drinks**.

miscarriage

Miscarriage in the cat is not common but is slightly more likely in the pedigree cat than the non-pedigree cat. Reasons for miscarriage are:

▷ stress: a fight with another cat, a fall, or any other extremely stressful situation can lead to miscarriage.

▷ infection: a bacterial or viral infection – for example a urological infection or the **Feline Leukaemia Virus** – will cause a cat to abort or give birth to weak or dead kittens.

▷ hormone deficiency: your vet may be able to give progesterone injections if alerted in time, as lack of this hormone

The Cymric, a longhaired form of the Manx (page 100)

can cause a queen to abort, usually between the 40th and 50th days of pregnancy. Unfortunately you are unlikely to know if your cat has a hormone deficiency until she has miscarried at this stage in several successive pregnancies.

If your pregnant queen has a dark-coloured discharge, get in touch with your vet immediately.

mitts

White markings on the dark feet of some cats, for example, the Mitted **Ragdoll**. Mitts are longer than **gloves** and shorter than **gauntlets**.

moggy

Moggy is used to describe a non-pedigree cat in the United Kingdom, and is a term almost unknown elsewhere. There are many conflicting stories of the origin of the word. In some parts of the United Kingdom any small, furry animal is known as a moggy. In Yorkshire, a mouse is known as a moggy; a cat is called a moggy there because it is a mouser. In Liverpool, moggy is said to be a corruption of margay, a small South American jungle cat. These wild cats were brought back to England by sailors who sold them to warehouse owners to control rats. Moggy could also be a corruption of mongrel, or Cockney rhyming slang, rhyming with 'cat and doggy'.

monorchid

A male cat with only one testicle descended. A monorchid cat may not be entered into a cat show in the United Kingdom as an undescended testicle will be retained inside the body and so attain a higher temperature than normal. This is considered a possible health risk by the registration bodies who do not want to encourage this fault (there is a high incidence of the retained testicle becoming cancerous). See also **cryptorchid**.

moulting

All cats will moult (shed hairs) in springtime in response, not to warmer weather, but longer days. Cats should be combed at least once a week but this is particularly important during the moulting season to prevent the formation of **hairballs**. Cats will also moult if they are ill and under stress, or old.

moving house

Moving house is almost as traumatic for a cat as it is for a human. Most cats are intensely territorial and find having their territory changed very distressing. You can make home-moving less stressful for your cat in the following ways:

▷ When the removal firm come to pack up and take your belongings away, lock your cat into an unused room, such as the bathroom. Give it food, water and a litter tray, and allow it to remain undisturbed until you are ready to leave.

▷ If you are moving your cat yourself, ensure it is placed in a secure container, to which it has become accustomed. If your cat is not used to travelling, take it for short trips in its carrier several times before moving. Make these trips as pleasant as possible, with catnip in the carrier and treats given at the beginning and end of the journey. A particularly nervous cat may need tranquillisers for a long journey; take your vet's advice on this.

▷ Some of the major removal firms have a special pet moving service which you might find useful. There are also firms which specialise in the moving of pets.

▷ When you arrive at your new home, place your cat in a room where it will not be disturbed. Again, the bathroom is probably ideal as no furniture will be moved in there. Provide it with all its comforts and make sure there is no way it can escape from the bathroom. When the removal firm have finished work elsewhere in the house, let your cat out of the bathroom.

▷ Allow your cat to explore your new home at its own pace. Remember to close all doors and windows and block off open areas such as fireplaces. It might help your cat to settle if you bring a litter tray containing used litter from your old home; it will smell familiar to your cat.

muzzle

The cat's chin and nose.

N

National Cat Club and Show

The National Cat Club was the first cat club to be formed in the United Kingdom. In 1910, after 13 years of existence, it amalgamated with the Cat Club to form the **Governing Council of the Cat Fancy**. Despite being the senior cat club, it is no more exclusive than any other club and anyone may apply for membership.

Each December the National Cat Club holds a one-day show in London. It is one of the largest of the British shows. In 1988 it attracted almost 2,000 cats and 15,000 spectators.

needles

Sewing needles often find their way inside cats and kittens because the needles have been left threaded. A cat is not interested in a needle but it is interested in thread, which it will play with, mouthing and chewing it. Once in its mouth, the backward pointing spikes on its tongue will prevent the cat spitting the thread out and it will have no option but to swallow it. If a needle is on the end, it will have to swallow that too. If you suspect that your cat has swallowed a needle, seek veterinary attention immediately.

nephritis

See **kidneys**.

nest-building

When a cat which lives wild is in kitten she will find a safe, secure place in which to give birth as the time draws near. Her 'nest' will not just be a place sheltered from the elements but somewhere which she believes will be safe from predators. So it is not surprising, when our domestic pets are in kitten, that they also try to find a nest in which to give birth safely. Often, this is the first sign the owner has that birth is imminent. As warm, dark, enclosed places are favoured, a cat will often choose to give birth in inaccessible or inconvenient places; in an airing cupboard or under a bed.

Life will be much easier for both the owner of a cat in kitten and the cat, if the owner provides a nest. The simplest is a clean cardboard box, lined with newspaper for warmth, with sheets of kitchen towel laid on top. Cover the box with a larger, upturned box with a hole cut in the side for access.

neutering/spaying

Neutering is the castration of a male cat to prevent it breeding, while spaying is the removal of the ovaries and womb of a female cat to prevent it breeding. Many owners become emotional at the thought of interfering with their cats' reproductive organs – feeling it is 'unkind' to do so. If you feel like this, visit any cat rescue shelter in the summertime and look at the dozens – if not hundreds – of unwanted kittens in every one of them. The kittens' mothers will probably be there too; cats whose only crime was to be naturally fertile and who have been thrown out of their homes because of it.

Even if you decide to let your cat have a litter or two and feel you are being responsible by finding homes for the kittens, remember that every kitten you find a home for deprives a kitten in a rescue shelter of a home.

It does not improve the health or personality of any female cat to be allowed to have one litter before spaying; in fact, having a litter of kittens can be painful, frightening, life-threatening and, for the owner, very expensive if things go wrong and veterinary attention is needed.

As for male cats, they are positively antisocial when un-neutered. They will spray their pungent-smelling urine all around your house, your neighbour's house, garden and car, in order to mark their territory. They will disappear for days (if not weeks) at a time in search of females in season, some travelling for many miles. They will fight other males for their territory and for the favours of the females and will return bruised and battered with ripped ears and injuries that will involve you in further veterinary expense. And one day your tomcat won't come back. In the excitement of the chase, he'll run in front of a car or, in a fight, he'll pick up a disease from an infected cat. Neutered males have a much longer life expectancy than entire males.

Males should be neutered at any time from four to nine months. At one time, male kittens were neutered at the earlier end of that range but now neutering is carried out as late as possible, to allow the kitten to develop fully, and, it is believed, to minimise the risk of

FUS. Spaying of female kittens is usually carried out between four and six months, although some vets are now carrying out the operation as early as three months.

nictitating membrane

See **third eyelid**.

non-pedigree

Non-pedigree cats are those whose ancestry cannot be traced. A non-pedigree cat can also be referred to as a domestic (mostly in the USA), a household pet (the name given to it at cat shows) or a **moggy** (a name unknown outside the UK).

Although each one is an individual, they have a definite 'breed personality' too. They have not been bred deliberately to exhibit qualities of friendliness towards people, so, although individuals may be extremely friendly, as a rule they tend to be more territory- than people-oriented. On more than one occasion when a house has been sold, a non-pedigree cat has been part of the deal, because the cat has refused to move.

This is not to say they make poor pets; the opposite is usually the case. Any owner who takes the time and effort to understand their non-pedigree cat is usually richly rewarded in terms of devotion, affection and lifelong friendship.

The non-pedigree cat is undoubtedly hardier than many pedigree breeds and is more resistant to illness and infection. Non-pedigree kittens mature earlier than their pedigree counterparts; they will wean earlier, start to play earlier and learn to use their litter trays earlier. As adults, they are often more streetwise than pedigree cats, better able to cope with traffic, dogs and unfriendly strangers.

In shape, size and colour there is a wide

Brown Tabby Norwegian Forest Cat and kitten (page 108)

range and variety. The non-pedigree cat can be found in virtually every colour combination, pattern and coat length. Longhaired non-pedigree cats, which form about 14% of the population, usually have silky, manageable coats, while shorthairs do a very good job of keeping themselves tidy and clean.

Norwegian Forest Cat   (see page 107)

Norwegian Forest Cats, also called Norsk Skogkatts, are big, healthy, hardy and strong cats. They love to play and are great climbers and excellent mousers. Intelligent cats, they love to show off and are very affectionate. Placid by nature, they accept other breeds of cats quickly when introduced into a catty household. They are slow to mature and are not fully grown until the age of 2½ to 3 years.

Forest Cat breeders report that kittens at birth have extremely long claws which they use to help their mother break the birth sac. They cling onto their mothers' fur when feeding and can be carried around in this way – an obvious boon to survival in the wild.

Their semi-long coats should receive regular grooming but, being silky, they don't mat, except possibly in the springtime when shedding (moulting). They have double coats; a woolly undercoat with a water and snow-repellent topcoat, which dries quickly when wet. In spring, the woolly undercoat is shed.

The breed is still popular in Norway where many are kept on farms for their mousing skills. They are believed to have originated from Asian longhaired cats taken to Norway by traders.

They are bred in a variety of colours and patterns and brown tabby is one of the most popular and attractive.

nose leather

The skin of the nose, which varies in colour from pale pink in white cats to black in black cats.

O

odd-eyed

Odd eyes, one orange (or copper) and one blue, appear only in white cats, shorthair and longhair. The parents of odd-eyed cats may both be blue-eyed, both orange-eyed or one may be blue-eyed and one orange-eyed. Odd-eyed cats are usually pedigrees but, occasionally, non-pedigree odd-eyed cats are born.

Odd-eyed cats are usually of good type with large, beautifully coloured eyes, so are often sought after for breeding. Sometimes, an odd-eyed cat is deaf in one ear; the ear on the same side as the blue eye – see **deafness**.

oestrus

See **season**.

offal

Offal is often fed to cats because of its cheapness, and, it must be said, because some cats adore it. However, owners would be better advised to spend their money on canned food, which is carefully balanced to provide all the nutrients a cat needs. Offal, no matter how much a cat likes it, is not a balanced food. A cat's natural food would be a mouse, or a rabbit, and if you examine the tiny liver, kidneys, lungs and heart of a rodent, you will see what a minute amount of offal a cat would be receiving in its natural diet. Therefore it should be a very small percentage of the amount we feed to our cats. 'Over-dosage' of offal can occur and it is dangerous.

▷ *Liver* has a high vitamin A content and, if fed to excess, can lead to hypervitaminosis A, which will cause pain in the joints and bony outgrowths which can cripple a cat. Unfortunately, many cats become addicted to liver, refusing to eat anything else. They *must* be weaned off their liver diet and tinned food can be useful here. 'Liver' flavoured tinned food, guaranteed complete nutritionally, can be fed daily without ill effects, as it may contain very little liver! Chicken livers have least vitamin A (12,000 International Units per 100 grams), calves' liver contains 37,500 iu, beef 53,000 iu and lambs' 75,000 iu. Liver should not form more than 10% or so of a cat's diet, and ideally should be less than that.

▷ *Heart* is almost useless nutritionally, and even dangerous. It is very high in magnesium and should not be given to any cat with urological problems (see **Feline Urological Syndrome**). In large quantities it is very hard to digest.

▷ *Melts*, also called spleen, can cause diarrhoea and are not recommended as a cat food.

▷ The *lungs*, known as lights, have almost no nutritional value and should never be fed to a cat.

▷ *Kidney* is less harmful than other offal.

▷ *Sweetbreads* are the thymus gland and, although they contain protein, they are high in phosphorus and potassium and lacking in vitamins.

When you cook offal, steam it in foil to retain the juices which should be fed to your cat with the meat. Offal can also be fed raw; many cats prefer it raw, while others will only eat it cooked.

oil in fur

If your cat has got engine oil on its coat, rub in margarine or vegetable oil. These combine with the oil and it can be removed more easily. Rub off as much as you can then bath the cat using a cat shampoo if possible. If not, use a pure mild soap, not detergent. Rinse thoroughly.

onychectomy

The technical name for **declawing**.

orange

A geneticist will call a ginger (red) cat orange or yellow.

Oriental Longhair

See **Angora**.

Oriental Tabby and Spotted (see opposite)

Havanas and **Foreigns** are referred to as Orientals in every country but the United Kingdom, where Orientals are the patterned versions of these cats. Their ancestry can be traced back to Siam (Thailand) where the original **Siamese** cats were bred in a variety of colours and patterns, not just the Himalayan or **Colourpoint** pattern we are familiar with.

The Oriental Tabbies have personalities similar to the other Foreigns; they are affectionate, active, playful and very intelligent.

Oriental Tabbies can have mackerel tabby markings. There is also an Oriental Spotted Tabby, whose spots may not always be very apparent to the non-expert. At one time, the Oriental Spotted Tabby was called the Egyptian Mau.

There are several, quite rare breeds of cat which have larger spots.

The *Ocicat*, with Siamese and Abyssinian ancestry, has large, clear spots.

A breed first heard of at the end of 1986, the *California Spangled Cat*, has large, clearly-defined spots or rosettes along its back and sides. Said to have some wildcat ancestry, these are extremely beautiful cats with a less Foreign look than the Orientals. They are said to be strong and active, yet gentle and affectionate.

outdoor runs

All cats benefit from sunlight. It synthesises vitamin D on their coats which they then lick off. Cats without access to sunlight may become deficient in this vitamin. Indoor cats which sunbathe through closed windows can also become deficient in vitamin D because ultra violet cannot pass through glass. Cats, like us, enjoy fresh air and they need some greenstuff to nibble on as an aid to digestion. All these things may be in short supply for the indoor cat, but there is an answer – an outdoor run.

An outdoor run will keep your cat safe from traffic, other cats and predators, while allowing it to enjoy sunshine, fresh air and grass, as well as the occasional insect to chase. Outdoor runs can be purchased ready made from

Oriental Tabby showing the lithe build of its Siamese ancestry

cat equipment suppliers. They can be as small as 6ft by 3ft by 3ft or they can be as big as your garden. The ready-made version will consist of a rectangular wooden frame with wire mesh covering it on all sides and top. A chalet to fit into this type of run can also be purchased, in case your cat is in the run when the weather turns wet or cold.

Portable pens can also be purchased. Made of sturdy wire mesh, they are intended for kittening but make excellent small outdoor enclosures, especially if the base is left off, allowing your cat access to grass.

If you have a small garden, you may find it as easy to fence in the entire area. Mesh fences – six feet high if local building regulations permit – can be erected around your garden with an 18-inch inward facing 'baffle' at an angle of 45 degrees to prevent your cat climbing out and others climbing in. The baffle must continue around any overhanging trees as a cat may try to climb a tree in order to jump over the fence.

Supervise your cat's outdoor sunbathing sessions at first, until it is used to its run. Ensure that there is always some shade for your cat and that it always has water available.

Don't leave your cat alone in its run for more than a few hours or it may become bored.

out of coat

During spring and summer months, when a cat is **moulting**, its coat may be sparse. This makes life particularly difficult for show cats, especially the longhairs (such as Persians) which are shown during this time, for example at the **Supreme Show** in May, as their coats will not be at their best.

ovariohysterectomy

Technical term for the spaying of a female cat. It means the removal of the uterus (womb) *and* ovaries.

overshot jaw

Some breeds, such as the Persian, bred with short noses and flat faces, may have an overshot jaw where the upper jaw is too long. This means that the upper and lower incisors do not meet in alignment – the upper teeth will protrude beyond the lower. If you are thinking of buying a Persian kitten, first look in its mouth to check its bite.

P

pads

A pad is the skin on the sole of the paw. Its colour corresponds to the colour of the fur; a white cat will have pink pads and a black cat will have black pads. Cats sweat through their pads.

paint on fur

To remove paint on fur, allow it to harden, making sure that your cat does not try to lick it off. Then, using blunt-ended scissors, carefully cut off paint and fur. Be very careful not to nick your cat's skin. This is really a two-person job; one to hold the cat still while the other trims the fur. The fur will soon grow back.

Don't use chemical solvents on paint in fur as it can burn your cat's skin badly.

panleucopaenia

See **Feline Infectious Enteritis.**

patched

A patched cat has clearly-defined patches of colour in its coat. For example, a tortoiseshell and white cat (also called a **Calico**) may have large patches of ginger, black and white fur.

pedigree

A pedigree cat is one which belongs to a breed which has been recognised by a registration organisation as 'breeding true'. That is, its offspring will look as it does, through three generations.

A pedigree certificate which lays out the animal's ancestry is given to the purchaser of a pedigree cat or kitten. It will include at least the cat's mother (dam), father (sire), grandams and grandsires, great-grandams and sires and great-great-grandams and sires.

peritonitis

Inflammation of the peritoneum which is the lining of the abdominal cavity. Peritonitis can be caused by penetrating wounds, a ruptured bowel or post-operative complications. See also **Feline Infectious Peritonitis.**

Persian   (see page 114)

These are the most popular of all the long-haired breeds and have **cobby**, solid bodies, broad heads and appealing round eyes. Sometimes referred to as the Longhair, these cats seem to have sprung up at around the same time in remote mountainous areas of the world such as Persia, Turkey and China.

Their fur is long with a heavy undercoat and a flowing tail, so grooming is vital. Don't consider buying a Persian unless you are able to find time to comb it *every day*. Five minutes a day is the minimum length of time taken to groom a Persian, but this varies with the individual cat's coat. Some are stickier than others and there are grooming powders

Red Self Persian, UK Champion (page 113)

and glosses which will help with difficult coats. Some owners spend 20 to 30 minutes each day grooming their Persians.

These are not ideal cats for the houseproud as moulting can be heavy and frequent. However, their sweet, gentle and placid natures will continue to keep the Persian among the most popular of cats. They are affectionate, loyal and loving towards their owners. Quiet-voiced, they are inquisitive and clever. Their calm nature means they are less de-manding than many other cats and they can settle down well with a working owner. They will not fret in a flat as access to a garden is not all-important to them, although indoor/outdoor Persians enjoy tree-climbing and hunting.

They are now bred in a wide range of colours: cream, white, blue, red, tortoise-shell, tabby and others. As the Persian type now requires small noses and large, round eyes, a few of these cats can have breathing problems or runny eyes. Choose your Persian – and your Persian breeder – carefully, to ensure you buy a really healthy cat.

The distinctive and beautiful Persian makes a loving and rewarding pet for anyone able to devote to them the time and care they require.

pet quality

A 'pet quality' pedigree cat is one which is, or should be, perfectly normal and healthy but not of breeding or show quality because it has a minor and unimportant imperfection, such as a spot of colour where it should not be or a longer nose than it should have, or a tail that is too long or too short. A pet quality kitten

should be less expensive than a breeding quality or show quality kitten. If you buy a pet quality kitten you will not receive its pedigree form until you have the kitten neutered (to ensure it cannot breed and pass on its minor 'imperfections') and arrange for a letter from the vet who neutered the kitten to be sent to the breeder of your kitten. This is standard practice to ensure that only the best kittens/cats are used for breeding – so do not take it personally!

pills, giving (see below)

Administering pills and tablets to a cat seems to cause more concern among owners than almost anything else. The reason is probably a

Handle your cat gently but firmly when giving it pills

simple lack of practice, as most owners have healthy cats which only rarely require medication. Approach pill-giving in a confident manner and it will be very much simpler.

▷ If you know from previous experience that your cat will resist strongly, **restrain** it by wrapping it in a towel or blanket. It will be a great deal easier if you have someone else to assist you by holding the cat, whether it is wrapped in a towel or not.

▷ You will find it easier to give your cat a pill if the cat is slightly 'off balance'. Rather than you getting down to the cat's level (which makes giving the pill more difficult for you) lift the cat onto a table. Cats dislike standing on smooth, shiny surfaces, they cannot get a grip and are at your mercy!

▷ Hold the cat's head with your thumb on one side of the jaw and a finger on the other and tip the head back. If the jaw does not drop open, place the nail of a finger of your other hand on the cat's bottom teeth and pull down.

▷ Drop the pill right at the back of the cat's mouth. Close the cat's mouth and gently hold it closed (making sure you don't cover the nose) until the pill is swallowed. To encourage your cat to swallow, stroke its throat, or touch the tip of its nose gently, or blow gently on its nose. You will know it has swallowed the pill when it licks its lips.

▷ If you have tried and really cannot master pill-giving, you will have to try subterfuge. Envelop a pill in cream cheese. Most cats love cream cheese and find it difficult to spit out because it is sticky. Or cut open a piece of meat, push the pill right into it, put the

'doctored' meat in a dish with other meat and hope for the best. If you are trying to hide a pill in this way, refrigerate the cheese or meat first which will help lessen the taste of the pill. If your cat enjoys yeast extract and the pill is of a type which you can crush (some must be given whole), grind it to powder and mix it with the yeast extract, put it on your cat's paw and watch while it is licked off.

pinch

A pinch is a fault in many breeds. It means that the jaw has not developed sufficient width, giving the face a 'pinched' look.

pinking up

Pinking up is usually the first sign of pregnancy. Around three weeks after mating the nipples of a queen in kitten will change from pale pink to deep pink and will become more erect and noticeable. Pinking up almost always occurs when a queen is in kitten for the first time; a queen which has had a litter may not pink up noticeably for second and subsequent litters.

play

Play is vitally important to a cat. Play starts in kittenhood, as soon as kittens are mobile – at three to four weeks. They will begin to play-fight with one another, and play with their mother's waving tail. This play teaches them much they need to know for subsequent survival. Play-fights among littermates teach a kitten how to defend itself and its territory and pouncing on moving objects is the first lesson in hunting for food.

In later life, play tones muscles and strengthens the cardiovascular system, and helps cats cope more easily with stress. And if you have regular play sessions with your cat, it will strengthen the bond between you. Play is particularly beneficial to kittens, older cats, indoor cats, cats under stress and will help tire over-active cats. Yet few owners ever think of playing with their cats on a regular basis. A regular play session can be fun for both cat and owner and do the cat as much good as an aerobics session for its owner.

Keep your play session to the same time each day, and not immediately after or before a meal. Spend ten to twenty minutes each day, starting and finishing with a gentle warm-up and cool-down.

There are many ways you can exercise your cat by play. Roll objects for it to play with, and, if the objects are oddly-shaped and roll erratically, your cat will enjoy it even more. Try: egg-shaped objects, pine cones, wine corks (especially champagne corks), plastic lemons, walnuts and plastic drinking cups, as well as table tennis balls, plastic practice golf balls and empty sewing-cotton reels. Also trail fabric for your cat to chase; a dressing-gown cord is ideal. Or make a fishing rod for your cat from a stick with strong twine secured to one end. Tie a piece of fabric or a catnip mouse to the other end of the twine and let your cat chase it, while you take it easy in a comfortable chair.

pleurisy

The lungs and chest wall are coated with a membrane called the pleura which can become inflamed, sometimes causing fluid to build up in the chest cavity. This pushes the lungs away from the chest wall, making breathing difficult. Pleurisy can be caused by bacterial or viral infections, sometimes after the chest has been damaged by, for example, a traffic accident. A cat with pleurisy may not show any signs until the condition is well advanced. It will seem generally unwell and off its food, with laboured breathing.

Antibiotics may be given and the cat should be encouraged to rest, perhaps by keeping it in a pen. Keep it warm and comfortable and feed it well. This is an illness where Tender Loving Care toward the feline patient will make a lot of difference to the outcome.

pneumonia

Pneumonia, meaning inflammation of the lungs, may also be caused by bacterial or viral infections, often after a chest injury, or after contact with an infected cat. Symptoms and treatment are similar to **pleurisy**.

points

The points are the dark colouring on a cat patterned by the **Himalayan gene**. There are nine points in the male: the mask, two ears, four paws, tail and the sexual organs; and, of course, eight in the female.

There is another meaning to the word points as in 'standard of points'. These were originally called 'points of excellence' and they were the characteristics which a cat of any breed should possess. See **standard of points**.

poison

There are many substances in our environment with which cats' bodies are unable to cope. They include such common everyday items as aspirin, paracetamol, phenolic compounds found in many disinfectants, and benzoic acid, a preservative used in many cooked meats. Cats may be given a poisonous substance by their owners, ignorant of the effects it will have, or eat a poisoned prey animal, they might fall into a poisonous substance, or walk on it, later licking their paws clean and swallowing the poison.

117

▷ Symptoms of poisoning can include any of the following: drooling, vomiting, breathing difficulties, depression, muscle tremors, diarrhoea, fits, staggering gait, loss of consciousness.

▷ Treatment: place your cat in a quiet, darkened room while you telephone your vet for advice. If the poisonous substance is known, take the container with you to the telephone, so that you can answer your vet's questions.

▷ It is best *not* to try to make your cat sick unless you cannot contact a vet immediately.

▷ *Never* make your cat sick if it has swallowed acid of any sort (including some cleaning agents and bleaches), alkalines (such as caustic drain cleaners and solvents), petrol, turpentine, paint thinners, dry cleaning fluid, flyspray.

▷ A salt water solution can be given if a vet is not immediately available, your cat is conscious, and has ingested antibiotics, anti-depressant tablets, aspirin, barbiturates, metaldehyde slug pellets or rat poison. Make the solution by dissolving two teaspoons of salt in half a cup of warm water. Give your cat at least two teaspoons of the liquid. Or place a small washing soda crystal at the back of your cat's tongue – it will immediately be sick.

▷ Prevention: treat cats like children! Keep all cleansers, bleaches and medicines firmly capped and out of reach. Never give a cat medicine which has not been prescribed by your vet, however innocuous it may seem. Do not give a cat dog medicine – it may be safe for dogs but potentially lethal to cats. If you notice a neighbour creosoting a fence, washing out a shed with Jeyes fluid or changing their car's antifreeze (all of which are poisonous to cats) keep your cat indoors. Do not give a cat chocolate, tobacco or alcohol – all are potentially lethal to a cat. Keep cats out of the room when decorating and keep them out of homes which have recently had chemical treatments, such as woodworm treatment. Use as few chemicals in your home as possible; restrict cleansers to diluted bleach, if possible, and allow to dry before cats are allowed into the room. Do not use waterproofing or stain-resisting sprays on your carpets or furniture. In the garden, store fertilisers and bonemeal in lidded containers, not sacks, be extremely careful in the use of insecticides and weedkillers (it is best not to use them at all) and, if you put down slug and snail pellets, place them under upturned flowerpots and weight them down with stones. As always, prevention is very much better than cure.

poisonous plants

The list of plants which are poisonous to cats is frightening in its length. However, many cats manage to live in households containing poisonous houseplants and where the garden holds untold hazards in the way of poisonous garden plants, without coming to any harm whatsoever. Although many plants are poisonous, cats are often too sensible to eat them. However, as cats do have to nibble a little **grass** or **green matter** as an aid to digestion, why take chances by providing green matter that is poisonous?

Poisonous indoor plants include: dieffen-bachias, poinsettias, castor oil plants, azaleas, daffodils, crocuses, hyacinths, chrysanthemums and mistletoe. Spider plants (*Chlorophytum*), although not poisonous in themselves, have been discovered by NASA, the US space agency, to absorb toxins such as carbon monoxide from cigarette smoke, and so to become poisonous.

Poisonous outdoor plants include: daffodils, crocuses, hyacinths, irises, lilies of the valley, chrysanthemums, philodendrons, yew, winter cherry, oleander, Jerusalem cherry, laurel, azaleas, rhododendrons, larkspur, mistletoe, foxgloves, lupins, laburnum, broom and monkshood.

polydactyl

Most cats have 18 toes – five on each of the front feet and four on each of the back feet. Polydactylous cats have extra toes. According to the *Guinness Book of Pet Records* the greatest number of toes found on a cat is 32, eight toes on each foot of a cat called Mickey Mouse which lived in California. Such cats can look as if they have 'double paws'.

Polydactylism is hereditary and is carried by a dominant gene, meaning that it can be inherited from only one parent. In the USA, it appears in certain areas. For example, about 15% of cats in the Boston area are polydactyls, a remarkably high percentage. It is sometimes said, incorrectly, that polydactylous cats do not appear in Europe. They do, but nowhere in such numbers as in Boston.

pot belly

If a kitten has a fat, tight stomach, suspect intestinal **worms**. Alternatively, it may be a sign of over-feeding.

prefix

A prefix is the cattery name of a breeder. Every cat she or he breeds will have her or his unique prefix, followed by the cat's given name. It's like a first name and a surname, only the other way around, because all cats from one cattery or breeder will have the same prefix. There are many rules surrounding the granting of prefixes, which vary according to the registration organisation involved. Sometimes a number of prefixes must be applied for, in order for one to be allocated, as no prefix, in any country, must be the same or similar to any other prefix. The **GCCF**, for example, also insist that prefixes should not be names of towns, counties or districts comprising a wide area, they should not be colours, names including colours, registered business or trade names, recognised titles, or 'any other word considered by the Executive Committee to be unsuitable'!

pregnancy

See **gestation** and **kittening**.

Premier

A Premier is the neutered male or female equivalent of a **Champion**.

pressure points

See **bleeding, external**.

prolapse

A rectal prolapse may occur after persistent diarrhoea, resulting in part of the bowel protruding from the anus. A prolapse of the uterus may occur after a difficult birth, resulting in the uterus protruding from the vagina.

In either case contact your vet immediately. Keep the prolapse clean and swab it with warm water on cotton wool. Apply liquid paraffin or petroleum jelly to keep it moist. Your vet should be able to replace the prolapse under anaesthetic if called immediately.

pulse

Each time the heart beats, a 'throb' is felt at the pulse points. To take a cat's pulse, place the tip of your middle finger, or middle and index fingers, on the inside of the thigh. The femoral artery which you will be able to feel there is the easiest place to take the pulse. When a cat is at rest, its heart will beat from 100 to 140 times a minute.

purring

Purring is not always a sign of happiness. A nervous cat will purr to show its anxiety and in a sick cat a purr can be a sign of pain. A queen will purr as a directional signal to her new, blind kittens; by following the sound they will find their mother and her milk. Cats which have suffered from respiratory infections often have rough, rasping purrs.

Purring involves both the throat and the diaphragm. Alternating activity of the muscles controlling the larynx and diaphragm causes a change in air pressure, creating vibration which makes the purring sound.

putting down, putting to sleep

See **euthanasia**.

pyometra

A condition of pus in the womb. Symptoms are discharge, thirst, loss of appetite and condition and vomiting. A cat suffering from pyometra must be spayed.

quarantine

Most commonly used to describe the period of isolation in which an imported cat is kept when it enters its new country to ensure it is free from communicable diseases such as rabies. The period of isolation varies according to the country of import as well as the country of export, but can be as much as six months for a cat entering the United Kingdom.

quarantine of a new cat or kitten

When you buy a new cat or kitten, even if it is purchased from a reputable source, it is possible it may be harbouring infection. Infection is passed so easily from cat to cat that, if you already own a cat, it is sensible to quarantine any newcomer until you feel sure it is completely healthy.

Keep it in a separate room with its own litter tray and food and water bowls. Ensure it has human company as any cat or kitten coming into a new home will be feeling a little lost and, if it has no company, lonely too. However you must be careful that your original cat(s) do not become jealous, so keep the newcomer company when the other(s) are out of doors. Or, if you can, have a friend or relative keep your cat(s) company while you play with the new one.

Wash your hands after handling the newcomer and before stroking your existing cat(s). Ideally, you should wear overalls or an apron when handling the newcomer, which you should leave in the isolation room.

A veterinary check-up is an excellent idea, even if the newcomer seems perfectly fit and well. Keep it in quarantine for at least three days if possible; five days to a week is better. Then introduce the newcomer to your cat(s) (see **introductions**).

queen

An entire female, used for breeding. Almost invariably used to denote a pedigree breeding female.

quick

The pink interior of your cat's claws. The quick contains nerves and will bleed copiously if cut.

R

rabies

Rabies is an often fatal disease which is endemic in most parts of the world. Only the United Kingdom, Australia, New Zealand, Hawaii and Scandinavia (apart from Finland) are currently free from rabies.

Protection from rabies is available by injection in countries where rabies is endemic and kittens can be vaccinated at three months with yearly boosters. Infection is spread when an animal or person is bitten by a rabid animal. If a cat has been bitten by a suspect animal, immediate treatment, using antiserum and vaccination, may be successful.

Symptoms include apprehension, personality change and dislike of bright lights and noise. However, by the time symptoms appear, the cat is already infectious and death is inevitable. It is therefore kinder, and safer, to have the cat put down immediately.

A human bitten by a rabid animal should wash out the wound thoroughly, apply antiseptic and seek immediate medical attention.

Ragdoll   (see opposite)

The beautiful Ragdoll has been badly served in many cat books. Because they are still relatively rare cats, few people have met one and this has allowed many inaccuracies to be perpetuated. The most common one is that the Ragdoll does not feel pain. In fact, the Ragdoll is quite normal. To prove this, in 1988 the British Ragdoll Club took the unusual step of having two Ragdolls examined by Dr Andrew S. Nash, BVMS, PhD, MRCVS, at the University of Glasgow Veterinary School. He concluded that 'these animals are normal members of the cat family.'

They are reputed to be the largest breed of domestic cat, with adult males reaching 15lb to 20lb (7kg to 9kg) in weight. They are slow-maturing cats, not reaching their full size for three or four years. There are three coat patterns in the Ragdoll. The Colourpoint has a coloured mask, ears, feet, tail and pads. The Mitted has the same points colours but white mittens on all four feet and frequently white blazes on their foreheads – a marking encouraged in the UK. The Bi-colour has a white inverted 'V' on the face with white legs and feet and points-coloured tail and ears. Ragdolls are bred in four colours: seal, chocolate, blue and lilac.

The name, Ragdoll, is said to come from the fact that a Ragdoll, picked up, will flop over your arms like a doll. In fact, they will only do so if they feel like doing so; like other cats they will wriggle furiously if they are not in the mood! They will usually lie on their backs in their owners' arms and have been said to be the nearest thing to a baby that a cat can be. They are relaxed cats although they show normal apprehension in strange places.

Ragdolls, showing the three coat patterns:
(left to right) *Mitted, Bi-Colour and*
Colourpoint

They are extremely affectionate and are great lapcats. Devoted to their owners, they will follow them around from room to room, settling wherever their owner settles. They will often answer to their name or to a whistle and will learn to walk on a leash. They have been described as somewhat dog-like, but puppy-like is probably a better description, because they are extremely playful and the kittens in particular can be very active.

They originated in California in the 1960s and are believed to be descended from a white longhaired cat, which may have been an **Angora**, and a **Birman** sire. **Burmese** blood may have been introduced in the early days too.

recognition

When a new breed of cat is being developed, its breeders will apply to a registration body for preliminary recognition for the breed. These cats can then be taken to shows where they will be judged against the standard of points provided by the breed club and merits awarded if the cats are up to standard. The breed may then attain provisional status and intermediate certificates can be awarded at shows. Once a registration body has accepted that the new breed *is* a separate breed of cat, the breed is recognised and the cats can attain championship status.

red

Pedigree cat breeders' term for **ginger**.

registration

The details of every pedigree kitten born are registered with a registration organisation. The breeder will send them details of the kitten's name, date of birth and ancestry. Anyone purchasing a pedigree kitten or cat should receive registration documents from the breeder.

rehoming cats

Unfortunately, there are many unwanted cats in every country of the world. In the United Kingdom alone, as many as 250,000 find their way into rescue shelters every year. These shelters are all overcrowded at certain times of the year, most especially in the middle of summer. This is because so many kittens are born in the spring and are old enough to go to new homes by summer and also because holidaymakers who have not made arrangements for their cat's care while they are away leave the cat to fend for itself.

These shelters are usually excellent places from which to obtain a cat or kitten. Even if a cat is brought into a shelter in poor health, it will be nursed back to the peak of health before being rehomed. Adult cats will have been neutered and inoculated by the shelters before rehoming. Sometimes special schemes are run by individual shelters to help provide older people on limited incomes with affordable feline companionship.

If you procure a cat or kitten at a shelter, you will not be able to take it home the day you choose it. You will be visited at home, by someone from the shelter, to ensure that you will be offering the animal a genuine home. If you are accepted by the shelter, you will either be asked for a donation towards the cost of the cat or kitten, or there will be a fixed fee, which may be waived in exceptional circumstances.

If you already have a cat which you can no longer look after for some reason, you may find it very difficult to find a shelter which will be able to take it, simply because there is usually a list of cats waiting to get in. So why not try to rehome it yourself? Advertise locally and enquire among friends and relations to see if they would like a cat or know anyone else who would. Don't forget to 'vet' prospective owners in the same way a shelter would.

respiratory disease

See **Feline Respiratory Disease**.

restraining a cat

It is sometimes necessary to restrain a cat, for

example, to give a particularly recalcitrant feline a pill. Do this by wrapping a towel around the cat in a firm roll, leaving its head and neck exposed but covering body and legs, so it is unable to struggle or scratch. If restraint is needed out of doors, for example, for an injured cat, wrap a jacket around the cat firmly but without making any injuries worse.

Rex (see page 48)

Rex cats are extrovert characters; extremely active and with a reputation for naughtiness. Ultra-intelligent, they are vocal in expressing their needs and will follow their owners around complaining if not given what they want. They become extremely devoted to their owners and are much more interested in people than territory, consequently they travel happily and will even go on holiday with their owners.

The Rex coat is basically an 'undercoat' with few or no guard hairs such as are found in other breeds. American, Cornish and German Rexes have no guard hairs at all, although the Devon Rex are said to possess a few guard hairs.

Rexes adore play and will retrieve objects thrown for them without any encouragement. They also enjoy riding around on their owners' shoulders. They are self-confident and unafraid and are consequently usually kept as indoor cats – allowed out they would probably go off happily with any stranger who played with them. They will learn to walk on a leash and can be exercised out of doors in that way.

Grooming is extremely simple as they have short, naturally curly coats which don't need brushing, although they might need an occasional bath. Their big **ears** can get dirty and may require cleaning once a week or so.

Although very skinny cats, they love food and seem to thrive best on several small meals throughout the day. They may not look it, but they are extremely tough little cats, although they can feel the cold and need a source of warmth during winter months. They love climbing into bed, between the sheets, with their owners and will also climb inside their owners' jumpers for warmth.

Rex cats can *sometimes* be suitable pets for those who suffer a *mild* allergic reaction to cats – but not always. Although their coat is very short, allergies may be caused by a number of factors (fur, skin, **dander**, saliva) and someone allergic to cat saliva will still be allergic to the Rex's saliva.

The *Cornish Rex* and *Devon Rex*, although similar in appearance, have descended from different natural genetic mutations. Devons have wider ears and they have **stops** to their noses, while the Cornish have a straight profile from forehead to nose. Although they have the slim body of the foreign-type of cat, they are all descended from ordinary domestic cats.

The first Cornish Rex was called Kallibunker and he was born in Cornwall in 1950 to a farm cat, and was the only curly-coated kitten in the litter. His owner had shown Rex rabbits and that was how the name originated. The first Devon Rex appeared in 1960 in Devon. Called Kirlee, his mother was an exstray which had probably mated with a curly-coated cat which lived in a nearby tin mine. However, the first recorded Rex was a *German Rex* which appeared in East Berlin in the mid 1940s. In various parts of the United States, a number of Rex mutations occurred at different times, and cross-breeding of the German and Cornish Rexes has taken place there.

Rex cats are bred in a very wide range of colours and coat patterns, including tabby and tortoiseshell. There is also a 'Siamese' version, the **Si-Rex**, which has the Rex conformation with Siamese points markings. In recent years, some longhaired Rex cats have also been bred, but these are rare.

ringed

Rings of colour on a cat's coat which run evenly along the tail or down the legs.

ringworm

Ringworm is a fungal skin complaint which may form a circular bald patch which looks scaly and dry on a cat's skin. Some types of ringworm produce a bald patch but the skin looks relatively normal. In mild cases, only a few broken hairs may be noticed. Veterinary treatment is needed to eradicate ringworm and will consist of an anti-fungal wash for the affected area and, in severe cases, a drug called griseofulvin will be prescribed. Ringworm is easily passed from one cat to another by means of spores which float in the air and which can live for up to 12 months. An infected cat should be quarantined from other cats in the household and its surroundings disinfected thoroughly. Bedding, grooming equipment, toys and scratching post will have to be burnt to prevent recontamination. Cats from a household in which ringworm has been diagnosed are disqualified from cat shows for at least four months after the owner's vet has certified the household as clear again. Cats can pass ringworm to humans, but it is believed that we are unable to pass it back to cats.

rubber bands

Cats love to play with, and chew, rubber bands. Some cats will chew them into pieces and swallow them with dire results to their intestines. Always keep rubber bands away from cats.

ruff

A ruff is the long hair around the neck seen in such breeds as the Persian. Can also be called a frill.

Russian Blue   (see opposite)

These elegant, green-eyed cats have sweet temperaments and quiet natures. They are friendly but not demanding. Their independence makes them very adaptable and they will not object to having a working owner, being well able to entertain themselves, but, being such friendly cats, they will enjoy a feline companion. They will also adapt to living in a flat. They enjoy family life and will be equally friendly with children and other pets. These affectionate cats have a great deal of charm and, with their loving ways, make excellent and intelligent companions.

The Russian Blue is equally happy in hot sunshine or in snow, in which they love to play. They can build up thick winter coats, especially if allowed out of doors, but once weekly grooming is sufficient.

Their origin is uncertain but it is thought they were first discovered at the Russian White Sea port of Archangel. Russian Blues are also called the Archangel cat, the Maltese, the Spanish Blue and the Blue Foreign. At one stage, the introduction of Siamese blood led to the development of a cat which was foreign in looks, like a Blue Siamese. Now the Russian Blue should once again resemble the early breed, except for the eye colour which has changed from gold to green.

The Russian Blue, a particularly elegant breed

S

salt-water (saline) solution

Dissolve one teaspoon of salt in one pint of boiled, cooled water to make a saline solution. This can safely be used to clean wounds or wipe eyes. Many **antiseptics** are not safe for use on cats.

sanction show

A sanction show is run on similar lines to a championship show but no challenge certificates are awarded.

schedule

Name, in the UK, for the entry form for a cat show, which also gives information about the rules under which the show is held.

Scottish Fold   (see opposite)

The Scottish Fold, originally bred in the United Kingdom, is now more popular in Europe and the USA. Opponents of the breed believe the folded-over ears impair the cats' hearing and are difficult to keep clean, perhaps leading to ear parasites and infections. Breeders of the Scottish Fold reject this point of view and say that the cats have good hearing and that the ears are no more difficult to clean than any others. The breed first appeared as a natural mutation in a Scottish farm cat's litter in 1961.

These cats are known for their good nature and sweetness. They have placid tempera-ments and, as they have round, chubby faces and **cobby** bodies, they are often said to be 'teddy bear cats'.

Grooming is simple as the coats are short and a once weekly comb should keep these unusual cats looking their best.

scratching

Perfectly healthy, flea-free cats will enjoy a good scratch from time to time. Scratching only becomes a problem if it is excessive. If you see your cat scratch, check the

▷ ears: If there is black material in the ears your cat may have ear mites. If there is an ear discharge there may be an infection. In either case, consult your vet.
▷ fur: If you can see insects or black specks (flea faeces), spray with an appropriate product, see **fleas**. If there is fur loss, there is a skin problem, see **eczema**.

scratching furniture (stropping)

Cats need to strop their claws. It keeps the claws in good shape, it helps mark a cat's territory with its scent and the stretching involved gives a cat an aerobics workout. So if your cat strops on your furniture there is no point in trying to stop it unless you provide it with something it *is* allowed to scratch.

*Tortoiseshell and White Scottish Fold;
compare her ears with the American Curls'*
(page 11)

Scratching posts come in all shapes and sizes, from the basic carpet or cord-covered upright on a base, to designer scratchers shaped like tortoises. Posts should be at least 30 inches (75cm) tall to allow your cat to stretch. Bases should be wide and heavy so that the post is stable. If it wobbles, your cat won't use it.

Some scratching posts incorporate shelves on top, which cats enjoy sitting on, and some have toys dangling from crossbars. Most scratching posts are upright but angled posts are also available and cats seem to like them.

Scratching posts can be home-made – and don't actually need to be posts. A scratching pad can be made by nailing or glueing a carpet offcut to an out-of-sight wall or the back of a piece of furniture. A kitchen table can have heavy cord wound around one leg for stropping purposes. And any do-it-yourselfer would be able to make a basic post on a stable base and cover it with glued-on carpet.

If your cat scratches the furniture, say 'no' in a loud, firm voice and remove it from the area. Place it beside its scratching post and, if it does not immediately use it, demonstrate! Run your nails down the post to show it what to do. Most cats are quick to use scratching posts when they are provided but if your cat is not one of them, rub some **catnip** into the post as an incentive. Remember to remove your cat every time you see it scratch the furniture, otherwise it will continue to do so knowing that it will sometimes get away with it.

seal

A dark brown fur colour which is sometimes so dark it can appear almost black, such as is seen on the **points** of the Seal-Point Siamese.

season

'Season', 'heat', 'calling' are all terms for the onset of oestrus – the time when a queen is ready to mate. The first season will occur at a different age for each cat but is often from seven to nine months of age. Usually, a female will start calling the first spring after she has reached six months of age. Foreign-type cats mature early, as young as four months, while longhairs mature later, at ten or eleven months.

Longer days and warmer weather encourage a female to come into season in spring. A queen mated in spring would bring up her litter in early summer, when the weather would be kinder to new-born kittens and there would be plenty of prey to support the new family.

The first sign that a female has come into season is usually a slight swelling of the vulva which she may lick frequently. She will then soon begin to call. Some pedigree queens have very restrained calls but most cats make quite a song and dance about it. They will roll around on the ground howling and an owner, seeing this for the first time, may think the cat is in pain. Vets are often telephoned by owners in a panic who think their cat has broken her back. If you stroke a calling cat's back, she will raise her pelvis and hold her tail to one side, as she would do if being mated.

Once calling starts, it will continue for between five and ten days. It will cease for two to three weeks, then begin again, lasting for five to ten days. After another two or three weeks, it will begin again, and so on. Theoretically this could continue throughout the summer, but in practice the female would find some way of being mated. Cats become extremely crafty when calling and will slip out of an open door before they can be stopped. And, as there is usually a congregation of tomcats sitting outside a calling cat's house, impregnation is almost inevitable.

If you have not got around to having your cat spayed, you will have to wait until the end of her first call before taking her to the vet. She cannot be spayed while in season as medical complications may ensue. In the meantime, you will have to bear with the noise and the tomcats waiting outside. Don't allow a cat to come into season time after time without mating. This can lead to cysts developing on the ovaries. Pedigree queens which are to be mated are usually mated on their third season, after they have called twice. After a litter, they are usually allowed to call twice before mating again.

self

A cat of all one colour; the same as solid.

sexing

To tell the sexes apart, lift the tail. Female cats have two openings closely set together. The lower opening, the vulva, is a vertical slit. In males, the two openings are further apart and the lower one is circular. In entire males, the testicles appear between the anus and penis. It is usually quite easy to tell the sex of new-born kittens as the bulge of the males' testicles is apparent. However, after a few days, the bulge may disappear making sexing more difficult until the kitten is mature.

shell

Hopefully you've never seen a pink elephant, but did you know there is a pink cat? The Shell Cameo Persian has a 'characteristic sparkling silver appearance, lightly dusted with rose-pink' according to the standard of points. From a distance, it looks white.

shock

Shock is the term used to describe the circulatory effects which arise as a result of severe trauma, eg road accident, massive blood loss or burns or toxins. In the early stages shock can be reversed, but if not treated will rapidly reach a stage where it becomes irreversible and therefore fatal.

▷ Symptoms: panting or rapid breathing, cold paws and ears, a dazed look with wide open pupils, pale or bluish gums, weak or rapid pulse.

▷ Treatment: keep the cat warm but not too hot. Wrap in a blanket in a warm room. Keep the cat calm with gentle stroking. Do not give the cat anything to drink by dropper or syringe. If the cat wishes to drink, give it sweetened water – *never* give a cat alcohol. If the cat does not begin to recover within a few minutes, take it to your vet.

shorthair

Felines can be divided into roughly two categories – longhair and shorthair. Long-haired cats, those which many of us refer to as 'fluffy', consist of 14% of the cat population. The remaining 86%, broadly speaking, are shorthaired (excluding those natural mutations such as the **Rex** which have only an undercoat and so hardly count as shorthaired, and the almost completely hairless **Sphynx**). Shorthair is much easier to care for than longhair, and so logically would be the natural coat length of the wild cat.

showing

Many owners don't realise that they can enter their cats, whether pedigree or non-pedigree, champion stock or not, in any cat show (with the exception in the UK of the **Supreme**). Only kittens under three months old, nursing queens, and entire non-pedigree adults cannot be shown.

Shows are held under the rules of one of the registration organisations. When you receive your entry form (called a schedule) the rules will be laid out within it. Send for your entry form several months before the show is to be held as the closing date for entries will be a month or more before the date of the show.

If entering your first show, choose one being held near your home. It will be less stressful for you and your cat if you don't have to travel far. Experienced show-cats learn to travel; many will travel hundreds of miles every other weekend to a show and in the USA 30,000 miles a year of show travelling is not unknown.

Ensure your entry form is filled in correctly as your cat may be disqualified if it is not. The name of the show manager will be printed on the front of the schedule; if you have any problems filling in the form telephone the show manager who will assist you.

Usually, a cat will be entered in one open class and three or four side classes. For a pedigree cat, the open class is its breed class, for example, Siamese, Birman, Turkish Van. For a non-pedigree cat, the open class is its colour, such as black, tabby, ginger. All shows have sections for non-pedigree cats, referred to as 'household pets'. Side classes you can enter may include, for example, debutante, for exhibits which have not been shown before, or fun classes for non-pedigrees such as 'cat with the longest whiskers'. Enter your cat for the minimum number of classes allowed if it is its first show, to allow it to get used to being handled by strangers. Cats which are not accustomed to showing can become cross with too much handling and judges don't like being bitten!

Your cat will spend the hours of the show in a pen and you will have to pay for the hire of this pen, sometimes called a benching fee, as well as paying for the individual classes you have entered.

Several weeks before the show you should receive a tally, a round disk on which is printed the number of the pen allocated to your cat. The tally is usually tied around the cat's neck with white ribbon. You should also receive a vetting-in card. All cats are 'vetted-in' at shows; a vet will check them over to ensure they are healthy and have no parasites. Any cat failing the examination will not be allowed to compete. You must take your cat's up-to-date vaccination certificate to the show.

For the show you will need a cat carrier, a blanket for the bottom of the pen, litter tray and food and water bowls. For some shows, blanket, tray and bowls must be white and the pen cannot be decorated in any way. Also take some food for your cat and a bottle of water, as water can vary in different parts of the country. You will also need a grooming brush or comb and some tissues in case eyes or bottom need a wipe.

You should have been **grooming** your cat regularly (probably daily) for some time prior to the show and also ensuring that its nutrition was top-class so that it will look healthy and at its best on the day. Remember that any grooming powders used must be completely removed from the coat or your cat may be disqualified.

You will have to be at the show hall early, an hour or so before it is open to the public, to vet-in your cat and settle it in its pen. Your cat will have to stay there until the show closes as no cat can be removed before the end of the show.

Rules for judging vary according to the body which has licensed the show. At some shows you will have to leave the hall, or stand at the side, while judging is carried out.

Female Seal Tabby-Point Siamese (page 134)

Judges and stewards will go from pen to pen taking out one cat at a time and assessing it. At this type of show you will not know how well your cat has done until a rosette appears (or does not appear) on its pen. At other shows, ring judging has been introduced. The cat is taken to the judge who stands behind a table and discusses the exhibit in front of an audience of exhibitors and visitors.

If you are a visitor to a cat show, remember that you must not touch any of the cats. Infection can be passed so easily from cat to cat by touch that this is strictly forbidden.

If you are an exhibitor you will realise that

showing is hard work and quite expensive too. There is no prize money, although pet food companies donate food, bowls or trophies as prizes at some shows. There is no financial incentive for non-pedigree cat owners to show. Only pedigree cat breeders will get some sort of monetary return eventually; kittens with champion ancestry will have a higher market value than those without. All winners receive rosettes worth a few pence but, more important than the prizes, is the satisfaction of having a 'top cat' – if only for a day. But beware, if you go to a show and your cat does well, you could become addicted!

show quality

If a kitten is sold as show quality (or show potential) it should conform closely to the standard of points for the breed, that is, it should be a good specimen of that breed. If you are planning to buy a kitten for showing you should first familiarise yourself with the breed's standard of points and visit some cat shows so that you will know a good specimen when you see one. Some breeders' standards, when selling 'show' kittens, are lower than others!

Strictly speaking, these kittens should be said to have show 'potential' rather than being of show 'quality'. No-one can really tell how a kitten will develop. A beautiful three-month old kitten can grow up to be a scrawny, gangly adult while the runt of the litter may become a show stopper.

Siamese   (see page 133)

Although these are the most popular short-haired cat in the United Kingdom, with 10,000 new Siamese kittens being registered each year, they are not the ideal cat for everyone. They are extremely demanding, often acting like jealous lovers if they do not receive enough attention. They are very vocal – that is, noisy – and like nothing better than holding long conversations with their owners. Their voices can sound like crying babies and, if a cat is in a talkative mood and their owner isn't, the Siamese wail can be irritating. Siamese queens on call make noises that have neighbours threatening to call the police.

The breed is thought to be at least 400 years old, and originated in Siam (now Thailand). The first Siamese were kept as pets by the ruling classes in their palaces and temples. The Siamese cat's looks have changed drastically over the last twenty or thirty years. The Siamese used to be an apple-headed, chunky cat but now they are extremely slim with wedge-shaped heads and large, wide-spaced ears. Many cat lovers believe the modern Siamese is too extreme in type and mourn the passing of the 'old-fashioned' Siamese which they say was healthier and longer lived. It is still possible to find an occasional kitten of the old-fashioned type but now this would be sold as a pet, not for breeding.

All Siamese have the typical creamy body colour with darker points. Born white, as are all cats coloured by the **Himalayan gene**, their colour starts to show within a few days and they continue to darken throughout their lives. Seal and Chocolate-Point Siamese are well known but less well known are the red, blue, lilac and tabby-points. Grooming is simple and **hand grooming** is often enough to remove any loose hairs.

These extroverted cats adore company and should have a feline companion, preferably another cat of foreign type, as well as plenty of attention from their owner. Siamese are extremely clever, quickly learning how to get their own way, how to open refrigerator doors and help themselves to the contents, and how to walk on a leash. They are great 'stroppers' so a scratching post is absolutely essential, along with some early lessons in using it. Curtain climbing is also a favourite Siamese activity, though a climbing frame may help here. Some Siamese have an even more destructive tendency – fabric eating (see **eating disorders**).

Although not the ideal cat for everyone, those who like the Siamese breed would not swop their clever, active, agile, inquisitive, naughty, almost-human cats for any other breed.

Singapura   (see page 136)

The Singapura is the native cat of Singapore – Singapura being the Malaysian name for the island. They have been called 'drain cats' as many were reduced to scavenging and living in drains because of the indifference of their countrymen. These narrow homes and their early inadequate nutrition probably account for their small size – the Singapura is reputed to be the smallest breed of cat.

They are brown cats marked with the lightest of tabby patterns, the hairs being ticked with darker areas on the back, legs and tail. Their lighter underparts are said to be the colour of unbleached muslin. Big eyes and ears are the breed's most distinctive features.

Introduced into the USA in the 1970s and the United Kingdom a decade later, these friendly cats are beginning to come into their own. They are adaptable, as you might expect given their early history, and are said to be very responsive to their owners' moods. They are extremely curious, wanting to investigate anything new, and join in whatever their owner is doing.

sire

This kingly title is given to the father of a cat and is only ever seen on pedigree forms.

Si-Rex

Short for Siamese-Rex, these are **Rex** cats patterned with the **Himalayan gene** which gives them the light body colour and darker points of the **Siamese**. In temperament, they are a mixture of both Siamese and Rex.

Smoke

A cat with a white or silver undercolour and a darker topcoat, blue or black, for example. On paws and face the hair is coloured to the roots.

sneezing

Sneezing in a cat should never be ignored as it may be an early symptom of a potentially fatal and very infectious illness, such as **Feline Respiratory Disease**. Should you be about to place your cat in a holiday cattery and notice an adjacent cat sneezing, you would be well advised to ask for a veterinary report on the sneezing cat, or to remove your own cat from the premises. Neither is easy to do, especially if you are just about to go on holiday, but nursing a cat with cat 'flu isn't easy either and that is what you may come home to.

Sneezing can have less serious causes; a mild viral infection similar to the common cold in humans, an allergy, or a foreign body in the nose.

Snowshoe   (see page 137)

Snowshoes are sometimes erroneously said to be shorthaired **Birmans** but those in the USA were developed using **American Shorthair** and Oriental ancestors. Snowshoes in the USA may only have points of seal or blue but the European Snowshoes may have points of any colour with white spotting on the muzzle and feet. The body colour is even in tone, lighter underneath. Eyes are large and blue.

The little Singapura, the native cat of Singapore (page 135)

These unusual cats have a striking personality and are very affectionate towards their owners. They enjoy company and are very adaptable, fitting in well in almost any home.

soiling

Nothing upsets owners more than cats which urinate or defecate where they shouldn't, on floors or furniture, instead of where they should, out of doors or in their litter tray. Often, the behaviour is misunderstood.

Owners think their cat is being spiteful and getting its own back after some slight. Or they think the cat has become lazy or is just plain 'dirty'.

It is important to realise that cats never soil their homes because of spite, laziness or dirtiness. A cat which soils its home is telling its owner that something is wrong. An owner may feel that this is an inappropriate way of pointing out a problem but, if you think about it, how else could a cat do so?

It is pointless and cruel to chastise a cat for soiling and will only make matters worse. A shout or a smack produces stress and stress leads to soiling, so it becomes a vicious circle.

The main causes of soiling are:

▷ illness. **Feline Urological Syndrome, cystitis** and impacted anal glands (see **anus**) are some illnesses which might lead to soiling. FUS can be life threatening and soiling may be the only symptom you notice. So, if your cat soils in your home, see your vet without delay.

▷ stress. Cats are creatures of habit and hate having their routine changed.

Owners on holiday, an addition to the family, a change of residence, someone leaving the family, an illness, all cause stress which may lead to soiling. Kindness and patience and time spent with your cat will help here.

▷ lack of litter tray. All cats should have a litter tray because there will be times when they are 'caught short'. No-one nowadays would dream of buying a house if it had only an outside toilet yet many owners expect their cat to go out of doors in all weathers.

▷ dislike of the litter or tray provided. Cats have their preferences about litter and should be provided with a type

The Snowshoe's blue eyes are a striking feature of the breed (page 135)

they like and will use. Some will not use litter if it has deodorising additives. Wash out the tray regularly in a diluted solution of household bleach; some cats will refuse to use trays which smell of pine **disinfectants** and most cats will not use a tray which is dirty or smells.

▷ confusion. If a cat 'covers up' faeces in its tray but has its paws outside the tray it may become confused by the feel of the flooring underneath and later use that flooring to eliminate on. Or if you move the tray, your cat may continue to use the place where it used to be. In both cases, a sheet of plastic spread on the area should help as cats dislike the feel of plastic under their paws.

▷ allergy. Some cats which have begun to soil stop when their diet is changed. They may be allergic to additives in some types of manufactured cat food although the same food will have no effect on other cats. Or soiling may be a reaction to something in their environment such as a carpet-cleaning solution or fresh paint.

▷ territorial marking. Soiling, both defecating and urinating, is a way of marking territory. A cat may begin this behaviour if it feels threatened in some way, perhaps by a new cat coming into the household. Give each cat its own 'territory', for example, allow them separate 'bedrooms' at night and this may help.

▷ old age or hormonal changes. An elderly cat has not the same control over its muscles as it once had and accidents will happen. Provide a litter tray on each storey for the elderly cat. Many queens, when they come into season, will urinate indiscriminately. If you find the soiling a problem, the queen will have to be spayed. Otherwise, you will have to live with it.

Whatever the cause of soiling, the soiled area must be thoroughly cleaned or the smell will trigger the cat to soil the area again. Wash the area with a weak solution of household bleach and water (test for colour fastness first). To eradicate smells completely, sprinkle the washed area with baking soda. When this is completely dry, vacuum it up.

Deterrents can be used but have limited effectiveness. Try a rinse of vinegar and water, oil of peppermint, citrus oils, a spray of perfume or pepper. Or a sheet of plastic or even your cat's feeding bowl placed on the washed area will discourage further use of it as a toilet.

solid

A cat of all one colour; the same as self.

Somali   (see page 141)

Somalis are basically **Abyssinians** with long hair. The earliest Somalis were probably produced by mating Abyssinians with **Persians** but they are now a breed in their own right.

They make endearing companions with their gentle and loving natures. They are bright, alert – and nosy. They want to investigate everything and will rush to the door when the bell rings to see who is there. They are lively cats and love to romp and play. Strong and healthy, they are very bold and love children. They are very 'catty' companions with their trusting, placid yet highly-intelligent natures.

Somalis need little grooming. Their hair, though long, does not mat and occasional brushing is enough to remove any dead hair. Colours are as for the Abyssinian and it takes

Somali kittens some time to develop the adult **ticking**.

Spanish Blue

See **Russian Blue**.

spaying

See **neutering**.

Sphynx   *(see page 33)*

The Sphynx must be one of the strangest – and rarest – cats in the world. A mutation in a litter of kittens born to an ordinary black and white cat in Canada in 1966 produced one hairless kitten. A Siamese breeder saved the kitten, which would probably have been rejected by its mother, and later mated it with its mother to found the breed, originally known as the Canadian Hairless.

The Sphynx is not totally hairless as it has short, fine hair on the back, head, ears and tail-tip and kittens are born covered with fine hair which disappears later. The hair on the face should feel like moss. A completely hairless Sphynx would be disqualified from a show because shaving would be suspected! The kittens are very wrinkled, as if they are wearing skin several sizes too large for them, but they grow into it and the adult cats are mainly wrinkled around the head. In fact all cats are wrinkled but this is usually hidden by the fur.

Their skin is pink where the fur would have been white and grey where it would have been black. Their bodies feel like warm suede, but they don't like being stroked as it is uncomfortable for them – patting is better. They have to be kept out of the sun in summer or they burn and they require a source of heat in winter.

They are very strong and muscular cats, extremely agile, with a love of climbing and playing. They have healthy appetites. They are very friendly, making a fuss of everyone they meet, and will settle down immediately in strange surroundings. Their breeders say that the Sphynx is the only breed of cat which can smile and that their toes are so long that the cats can use them, monkey-like, as fingers.

There are only a very few breeders of the Sphynx in the world and, as the cats do not appear to be prolific breeders, they may never exist in great numbers. Despite an enormous price tag (£4,000 per cat in 1989) breeders rarely part with their kittens, preferring to keep them for themselves.

The Sphynx is not the first hairless breed. The Mexican Hairless appeared in the 19th century, but the breed died out within a few years.

spraying

Spraying should not be confused with urination, although a cat uses urine to spray. However, a cat will squat down to urinate but stand to spray, backing up to a vertical object and spraying a jet of urine backwards. Both males and females spray, whether neutered or entire, but males are more likely to spray, especially if entire. It is the male hormone, testosterone, which can trigger spraying behaviour.

Spraying is mainly territorial in origin. It is a pungent way of marking territorial boundaries to let other cats know who owns a particular patch.

If your cat sprays:

▷ is he neutered? It is important to have a cat neutered before spraying becomes a habit which will be hard to break later. Some cats continue to spray after being neutered because some testicular tissue has been left behind. This continues to produce testosterone and the cat continues to behave like an entire tomcat. Remaining tissue can be removed surgically or hormone levels can be adjusted by a course of drugs.

▷ does he believe his territory is threatened? If a new cat has been introduced to the household he may be feeling under threat. Several cats living in one household should be allowed their own 'space', perhaps by having separate sleeping quarters. Most spraying problems seem to arise when the 'danger number' has been reached – four cats in one household. Or your cat may be reacting to an outside threat. Is there a neighbourhood cat which is spraying in your cat's territory? If so, try to chase it away.

▷ is your cat under stress? Cats can become stressed by change of any kind in their routine. A new pet or baby, a change of residence, a holiday, even a change of feeding area, can be enough to set off spraying behaviour. If spraying has been caused by a change in the household and the change is reversible, then change it. Otherwise you will have to be patient and understanding until your cat gets used to the change and stops spraying.

▷ does an unspayed female live nearby? If she comes into season, she could cause your cat to spray, even if he is neutered.

Male cats kept for breeding will spray as a matter of course. Most breeders keep their studs in outdoor runs where they will spray to their heart's content and not bother anyone, but some keep their studs indoors and have to learn to live with the smell. If all else fails, it has been known for the owners of a spraying cat to accustom it to wearing a baby's nappy – with a hole cut out for the tail to go through!

squint

A squint, also known as *strabismus*, is a positioning of the eyes so that they both look towards the nose or else look in different directions. It is a not uncommon fault in the Siamese and some people believe the squinting cat sees double. It will deliberately squint in order to correct this handicap. There is, of course, an ancient legend to account for the Siamese squint. They were said to have been charged with guarding a very valuable vase by temple priests. They watched it with such concentration that their eyes became – and stayed – crossed.

standard of points

A standard of points is a blueprint for a breed. It lays down what the ideal cat of that breed should look like. It is drawn up by the committee of a breed club and accepted by a registration organisation which then uses it to judge all cats of that breed.

Cats sold as show quality should conform closely to their breed's standard of points, breeding quality cats may have one or two variations from the standard and pet quality kittens may not conform very closely at all.

staring coat

When a cat's coat is lustreless and rough-looking, it is said to be 'staring'. It is a symptom, sometimes the first, that a cat is unwell. Commonly, it is caused by the presence of intestinal worms or skin parasites or by a nutritional deficiency. It may also be a symptom of a more serious illness so check with your vet if in any doubt.

A Usual or Ruddy Somali (page 138)

stop

A stop is when the nose, rather than being straight from skull to nose tip (as in the Cornish Rex) has a dip in the middle (as in the Devon Rex).

strays

It is a moot point whether or not there is really such a thing as a stray cat. In all my years with cats, I have never known one 'stray'. I have known a few which moved next door when living there appeared more comfortable than at home. And I have come across many which have been abandoned when they grew up and were no longer cute, or became pregnant. But there is no reason why a cat, a creature of habit, would leave a comfortable home to live elsewhere. Only when the home is not comfortable would a cat move.

So if a 'stray' appears on your doorstep it is very important to make sure that it *is* a stray before taking it indoors and keeping it there. Many 'strays' are just chancing their luck; they have a good home but their owner may be out at work. They feel like company and a good meal so they go off in search of a neighbouring cat lover. Many cats have acquired two homes in this way; their original home where they live in the evenings and at night and a new daytime home where they are fed and cossetted and traditionally (but wrongly) let out to 'roam' at night. Neither owner is aware of the other and both are astounded at the duplicity of 'their' cat should they ever find out.

Other stories are sadder. A cat, begging for an extra meal, is taken in by a kind-hearted person who decides it is a stray and keeps it indoors for the next few weeks to accustom it to its new home. In the meantime, its real owners are frantic looking for their lost cat. So if a sad-eyed 'stray' appears on your doorstep, check it over before you fall for the excellent acting of the average moggy.

▷ is it really thin? If you can feel its ribs and backbone it has probably not eaten for several days.

▷ what shape is it in? If its paws are rough or torn it has possibly walked a long distance. It may have stowed away on a lorry and be making its way home.

▷ what can you do? You can feed it if it is hungry and give it water to drink. If it has parasites such as fleas, you can spray it. You can make sure it has an *outdoor* shelter from the wind and rain which it can leave any time it wants. But before you take it in, make very sure it *is* a stray. If it isn't and the owners claim it back, you can have a lot of heartache.

Advertise locally in newspapers and shop windows. Place a collar around the cat's neck (a paper collar if you are worried about safety) with a message on it saying that you believe the cat is a stray, but, if not, will the owner contact you. Give your telephone number. Inform neighbours, pet stores and vets that you have the cat.

And, if after all that, an owner fails to turn up, you can safely assume that the cat, if not a stray, is at least homeless. Except, by this time, the cat probably isn't homeless – is it?

stud

A stud is an entire male cat used for breeding purposes. He will lead a very specialised life, usually living in stud quarters in a garden (because he will spray). Some owners will only let their stud cats service their own queens while others are at public stud. Their owners will be choosy about which females to accept; if they don't know the female's owner they will ask to see the cat's pedigree and other documentation, and will refuse any female which they feel is not up to standard. If they accepted females which were not up to standard, the kittens would probably be inferior in type too and this would rebound on their stud. So the non-pedigree cat owner's dream of finding a pedigree cat to sire kittens is just that – a dream. No reputable stud owner will allow their cat to mate with a non-pedigree cat, however pretty.

Stud cat owners have certain responsibilities. They must ensure that their stud is tested regularly for **FeLV** and that he is in good health. They should ensure he is not used too often and that his stud house is cleaned and disinfected between each visiting queen. Stud owners should supervise matings to ensure that mating does take place and that a nervous or inexperienced queen is helped, if necessary. In return for this, they receive a generous fee; several hundred pounds in some cases. They should not only hand back a healthy, happy, pregnant queen to her owner, but also a mating certificate giving details of the stud's ancestry. If the mating hasn't 'taken' and the queen isn't pregnant, they should give a remating, without further charge.

If you are the novice owner of a breeding queen, join the appropriate cat club and take advice from the members about the stud to choose. Ask to see pedigree forms, to ensure the two cats' backgrounds are compatible and, if you are not sure, get in touch with someone senior in the club and ask for advice. Everyone loves giving advice and cat people can be extremely knowledgeable and helpful. Remember that people in a breed club have the interests of the breed at heart and really want to help novice breeders make the right choice so that any kittens which result will be of as good quality as possible.

stud tail

Entire males may suffer from stud tail. It is an oily secretion at the base of the tail giving a greasy patch which can become infected. Daily shampooing may be necessary, especially in the breeding season. If shampooing is not carried out, infection may result and antibiotics may be necessary. Cats which are not required for breeding purposes should be neutered, in which case stud tail will not occur.

Supreme Show

The Supreme Cat Show, held in the UK during May, is the only show where cats must already have won a **challenge certificate** in order to compete. It is held by the **GCCF** and is the feline equivalent of Crufts. It is probably the most interesting cat show in the UK, from the visitor's point of view, as the cats on show are the top cats in their breed and their pens are decorated by their owners in the most creative and imaginative ways.

T

tabby
(see opposite)

Tabby is the name given to striped cats, most often 'grey' and black, although tabbies are now bred in many other colours including silver, brown and red. The grey colour seen in some tabby coats is, in fact, composed of bands of black, brown and yellow, producing the optical illusion of grey, and called **agouti**.

The name of the tabby is said to have come from Attabiy, a part of old Baghdad. Watered silk was produced there and its wavy pattern was very similar to the wavy stripes of the tabby cat. Perfect tabby markings should include 'bracelets' on the legs and rings around the tail, as well as an 'M' on the forehead.

tapetum lucidum

The tapetum is a light-reflecting layer at the back of a cat's eyes which acts as a 'gatherer' of any available light. The cat's pupils dilate in the dark to let in as much light as possible, and this can be seen reflected back from the tapetum in the light of a torch or car headlights. Usually cats' eyes shine green or yellow, but some cats' eyes shine red, which may mean that these cats lack a tapetum and consequently see less well in the dark.

tapeworms

See **worms**.

tartar

Tartar builds up on the teeth if they are not kept clean and 'exercised'. In the wild, the biting and shearing of prey meat keeps the teeth clean but domestic cats, raised on a diet of soft, processed food, often suffer from a build-up of tartar on the teeth where they enter the gums. This can lead to inflammation (**gingivitis**) of the gums when bacteria enter the tooth socket and can lead to loss of teeth.

Prevent tartar build-up on your cat's teeth by feeding a little dry food daily and by giving a chunk of raw meat at least every few weeks. See also **teeth**.

taurine

This is a substance similar to an amino acid which is essential in a cat's diet. A dog can synthesise taurine from two amino acids but a cat cannot, so it must be obtained directly from the food it is given. Taurine is found in meat and fish but not in vegetables, so cats cannot live healthily on vegetarian diets. Nor can they thrive on dog foods; this contains too little taurine for a cat's requirements.

Over a period of months or years, a cat fed on a taurine-free diet will suffer retinal degeneration and will eventually go blind. This was discovered only in 1975 and, even more recently, it was discovered that taurine is important for healthy heart function. Taurine

Female British Shorthair showing the black and silver tabby pattern

also has an important role in kittening: queens fed on a taurine-free diet had fewer kittens, many were still-born and fewer survived than kittens born to queens fed on a properly balanced diet.

teeth

Kittens' first 'milk' teeth develop during the first month of life. By around six weeks a kitten will have its full complement of 26 teeth. The permanent teeth begin to come through at about four months and a kitten's mouth may feel a little sore at this time. The milk teeth are pushed out by the permanent teeth and you may find one or two lying on the carpet, although kittens usually swallow them, with no ill effects.

Adult cats have 30 teeth; 4 large canines which hold and kill prey, 12 incisors between the canines wich are used for gnawing, and 14 back teeth (pre-molars and molars) which act like scissors, shearing meat into pieces. The teeth wear down with age and elderly cats may lose some teeth. This usually causes no problem as long as they are given soft food. Unlike horses, it is not possible to tell a cat's age from its teeth, although the amount of **tartar** may give a very rough guide.

Tartar build-up can cause problems but can be avoided if you clean your cat's teeth regularly, preferably weekly. First accustom your cat to having its mouth touched by gently lifting the corner of its lip while it is relaxing on your lap. Do no more than this at first until it becomes used to you touching its mouth. Then lift its lip and run your clean finger along its teeth. When your cat becomes used to this, try brushing, using a child's toothbrush or one of the toothbrushes specially made for animal use. Use it dry at first then try brushing with a toothpaste of baking soda and water or salt and water.

temperament

Few people realise that cats' temperaments vary with their breed and few stop to think about the temperament which would suit them best before they buy a kitten. Yet someone who enjoys a quiet life would be ill-suited to Siamese keeping, while an active extrovert might find a Persian too placid. So if you are thinking of buying a cat or kitten, first decide what sort of temperament you would like to live with – temperament is much more important than looks – then read the entries for the various breeds.

Bear in mind how a kitten has been raised; this often has a profound effect on temperament. Some kittens in large breeding establishments are raised in pens, rarely even seeing humans except at feeding and cleaning-out times. These kittens may be withdrawn and unfriendly. If they have had no human contact in the first few vital weeks they may even be frightened of people. Such kittens may never totally overcome their wariness. If you want a kitten as a pet, you should purchase it from a breeder who has raised it in a home environment, as part of the family, where it has had full rein to play and become socialised.

temperature

There is only one way to take a cat's temperature and it does not enjoy it any more than you do! Some cats object so strongly to having their temperatures taken that it should be left to the vet, in case the cat is hurt by inexpert attempts. The thermometer used should have a stubby end and not a thin, easily-broken one. Shake the thermometer to bring down the mercury and lubricate the end with petroleum jelly, liquid paraffin or vegetable oil. Very carefully, insert the thermometer into the anus, no more than two centimetres, and keep it there for about a minute.

A cat's temperature varies around 38.4°C to 38.6°C (101°F to 101.5°F). The temperature of kittens is usually a little higher than that of adult cats.

territory

Cats are territorial creatures – with good reason. A cat which had to find its own food would have access to any prey within its territory; by keeping other cats out there would be more food for itself. Entire tomcats will have very large territories – perhaps as much as 150 acres – while the territories of neutered pets will be much smaller. Nevertheless, the territory of a neutered male may be as much as six or seven times as large as that of a spayed female.

Sometimes territories will overlap and there will be shared areas, especially in urban environments. Some pathways through and between territories will be shared while others will 'belong' to specific cats, who will defend them.

Territories are gained, and retained, by fighting, so the biggest, strongest, most assertive cat stands to gain the best territory. Any newcomer to an area will have to fight to gain its position. This explains why cats, having moved home with their owners, are often loath to go out of doors at first; it is because they will have to fight to be allowed in their own gardens.

Territories are marked by their owners in a number of ways, including scratching tree trunks and fence posts and defecating in prominent positions. Very assertive cats do not 'cover up' after they have defecated. The most favoured territorial marker is spraying urine over vertical objects such as trees, fences, sheds and the wheels of cars. The cat will back up to the selected object, raise its tail and spray a jet of urine backwards. This is easier than it sounds as the male cat has a backward-pointing penis. Spraying will be repeated every few yards around the territory. Although spraying is most common in males, especially males which have not been neutered, females will spray too.

The sprayed urine has chemical markers which identify it as belonging to a particular cat and from it other cats can tell whose territory they are in. The strength of the smell of the urine disminishes as time passes, and this allows visiting cats to calculate if it is a 'current' territory – and one which is regularly patrolled – or one which is infrequently used or vacant. This may be why cats want to go out of doors frequently, even if they do not stay outside for long. They probably go out just long enough to renew their territorial markings.

theft

Approximately 93% of cat owners in the United Kingdom have non-pedigree cats so approximately 93% of cat owners in the United Kingdom think that their cat couldn't possibly be stolen. 'My cat has no value,' they say. 'It's only a moggy.'

In fact, that's a fallacy.

Pedigree cats are rarely stolen because stolen pedigree cats are valueless. They cannot be used for breeding as their offspring will have no papers – only the owner registered with the registration organisations can provide pedigree certificates and transfer certificates. And although many pedigree cats have beautiful fur, which might make good pelts for fur coats, matching pelts would be in such short supply that they would barely make a pair of earmuffs, let alone a coat.

Almost all stolen cats are non-pedigree cats

– and one particular colour group tends to disappear from an area in successive waves rather than continuously, suggesting that the cats may be stolen in an organised manner. Several markets have been identified by Petwatch, a charity which monitors the loss and theft of family pets. In Europe, the fur trade relies on cat fur for cheap coats. Gloves, handbags and fur toys are also made from cat fur.

Some pets stolen from the streets may find their way to experimental laboratories via unlicensed dealers. And a few are used in cat-coursing and possibly even witchcraft rites.

How can your prevent your cat being stolen?

▷ *Never* 'put the cat out at night'. Cats are much more likely to be stolen during the hours of darkness. Provide your cat with a litter tray, a warm bed and its last meal of the day and it won't even want to go outside.

▷ Keep alert. If you see a stranger in your neighbourhood with an unmarked van, take the number and report any suspicious sightings to your local police.

▷ Know where your cat is. Do you know if your cat is indoors or outdoors at this moment? If you have a cat flap, you may not. When you let your cat out, call it back indoors if it has not returned within fifteen to twenty minutes.

third eyelid

The third eyelid is more correctly known as the nictitating membrane or the haw. It appears at the inner corner of a cat's eyes and is sometimes a sign that the cat is unwell. If the third eyelid is visible, check with your vet.

However, sometimes the third eyelid is only a symptom of a loss of weight in the cat. The eye rests on a small pad of fat and if a cat loses weight, it may also lose fat behind the eyeball, leading to a sinking of the eyeball and the third eyelid becoming visible.

thirst

If your cat begins to drink more than usual a veterinary checkup would be in order as increased thirst is usually a sign of illness.

▷ Nephritis and kidney disease, often seen in the older cat, cause thirst and an increase in urination (see **kidneys**).

▷ **Feline Infectious Enteritis** appears to make cats thirsty but unable to drink.

▷ **Diabetes** causes thirst and increased urination.

▷ **Pyometra** will cause an affected queen to be thirsty.

▷ **Shock** is accompanied by thirst.

threadworms

See **worms**.

ticking

When two or three bands of colour are visible on one individual hair, this is known as ticking. The best-known ticked cat is the **Abyssinian**.

ticks

Ticks are blood-sucking parasites which are often found in long grass, causing a problem for any cat which roams in it. They bury their mouths in the cat's skin and hold on. As they become engorged with blood they become purplish in colour and increase in size. Don't try to pull them off as the mouth parts will be left behind and will set up an infection. Dab a drop of clear nail varnish on each tick; this

Tonkinese kittens (page 150)

makes them let go. Then use tweezers to remove them and burn them. Some flea sprays will also kill ticks; read the labels to find out which are effective.

Tiffany

A longhaired version of the **Burmese**.

tipping

Some cats have hairs which have a contrasting colour at the ends; this is called tipping. For example, the **Chinchilla** has white fur with black tipping which gives a sparkling silver effect.

toilet training

Toilet training is rarely necessary in cats. Kittens, as soon as they are able to climb out of their kittening box, usually make a bee-line for their litter tray. After they have eaten a little litter (and no-one knows *why* they eat it) they usually use it for its recommended purpose, without having to be trained to do so. As usual, non-pedigree kittens are quicker to learn than pedigree kittens, which usually have a few 'accidents' before they get the hang of it.

If your kitten needs help to learn to use a litter tray, place it on a tray containing clean litter after every meal. Scratch the litter with your fingers, which duplicates the sound of 'covering up', as this will often remind kittens of what they are there for.

Older kittens or cats which refuse to use their litter tray usually have a good reason for doing so; see **soiling**.

tomcat

A name given to any male cat but, more correctly, to a male cat which has not been neutered.

Tonkinese   *(see page 149)*

Tonkinese, which look like **Siamese**, are the product of a **Burmese** and Siamese mating, as opposed to the **Balinese** which is a longhaired Siamese which has appeared spontaneously in litters of purebred Siamese. When Tonkinese are mated, they can have kittens which are Burmese, Siamese or Tonkinese.

They seem to have the characteristics of both sets of parents, being extremely extrovert and clever. They are very nosy, wanting to know what is going on all the time and refusing to accept that anything – or anywhere – is out of bounds to them. Like their Siamese ancestors, closed doors are no bar – they soon learn to open them!

They are extremely affectionate towards their owners and they like another cat for company too. In feline company, they can be ringleaders in any mischief which is taking place. They can be self-willed but can be trained and will learn to walk on a leash. They are not as noisy as the Siamese and grooming is simple.

Torbie

A combination tabby tortoiseshell and white cat.

Tortie, Tortoiseshell

Tortie is the shortened form of tortoiseshell – a mottled or brindled ginger and black cat. Those with the most attractive markings do look like tortoiseshell – the polished shell of a tortoise. The introduction of the white spotting gene alters the appearance of tortoiseshell giving it a patched appearance and the colours appear in large patches of ginger, black and white or cream, blue and white. The gene which causes the colour is sex-linked and tortoiseshell cats are nearly always female. Tortoiseshell males are occasionally born; it is thought they are always infertile.

toxoplasmosis

Toxoplasmosis is an illness which is extremely common both in humans and in cats, but humans do not necessarily become infected via cats. Butchers and anyone who eats undercooked meat can become infected and in most western countries approximately half of the population has had toxoplasmosis at some time. It is usually a mild disease, similar to 'flu, and those who have been affected (often without knowing it) develop an immunity.

Cats which have toxoplasmosis may have no obvious symptoms but their faeces can be infective for up to five weeks. The faeces contains the encysted parasite *Toxoplasma gondii* which they acquire by eating infected prey, undercooked or raw meat or from the faeces of infected cats.

Pregnant women are most at risk from toxoplasmosis, but only if they have not been exposed to the disease before (and approximately half have and so are immune).

However, there is no need to get rid of the family cat. It can be tested for antibodies to toxoplasmosis. If they are present in the blood, and a further test a week later shows no increase, the cat has previously been infected and is now immune. Its faeces will not be infective and will pose no risk.

If the family cat possesses no antibodies, hygiene precautions can be taken.

▷ Pregnant women should delegate someone else to clean out the litter tray. Whoever does it should, of course, always wash their hands afterwards. Disinfect trays daily.
▷ Cook meat thoroughly, whether for human or animal consumption.
▷ Wear gloves if gardening and keep children's sandboxes covered.

toys

All cats – not just kittens – love to play with toys. However, there is no need to spend a fortune to keep your cat amused.

A favourite with most cats is the catnip mouse – and it need not be mouse shaped to be fun. If you have a scrap piece of fur fabric, cut it into two long strips, place right sides together and sew up three edges. Turn right side out, stuff with catnip, which you can buy from some pet stores and health food stores or herbalists, turn in the unsewn edges and sew up the seam. The tube-shaped mouse works very well as it will bend and flop in the middle, allowing your cat to toss it around but, if you are a purist, you can make a mouse-shaped mouse from two triangles of fur fabric. A strong, non-fraying piece of cord can be attached securely at one corner to become a tail but don't make eyes, nose or mouth as they can come off and be swallowed.

Safety is very important when choosing toys for your cat. Choose them as carefully as you would choose toys for a baby and bear the same safety rules in mind. Some cats' toys are dangerous, with loose pieces which can come off and choke a kitten. Make your own toys but, if given toys as presents, try to tear them apart. If they come apart in your hands they will certainly come apart in your cat's mouth.

Cats enjoy chasing rolling objects, so table tennis balls and practice golf balls (the plastic type with holes in) provide hours of fun. You could place one of these balls in a large box or in the (empty) bath and your cat will enjoy batting it around inside. Or place it in a shoe box which has had the lid taped shut and several paw-sized holes cut in it. Your cat will try to catch it through the holes.

Objects which are usually thrown away make good cat toys, for example, empty plastic lemons or eggs, wine corks and sewing cotton spools. String several cotton spools together and leave them dangling from a door handle or the back of a chair.

Don't forget the humble cardboard box or brown paper grocery bag (not plastic, which can suffocate). Leave either sitting in the middle of the floor and your cat will enjoy hiding inside and pouncing outside. Just like children, you can spend a lot of money on buying the newest line in cat toys, only to discover that your cat's favourite plaything turns out to be the box the toy came in!

training

Yes, cats *can* be trained. Few owners are interested in training their cats to do tricks, although one American feline can jump fences on command, shake hands with strangers, sit up and beg, play basketball in a scaled-down court and play *Three Blind Mice* on the piano. However, most owners would like to train their cats in the rules of their household so that they can live together peacefully.

It is important to start early and to start as you mean to go on. As soon as your new kitten has settled down, teach it the rules of the household. It is vital that you are consistent. If it strops on the furniture, say 'no' in a firm voice *every time* and carry it over to its scratching post. If your cat is allowed to strop furniture sometimes you will never stop the habit. So tell it off every time you see it stropping and remove it. You must provide a scratching post, however, as cats do need to strop.

If you do not want your cat to sleep on your bed for the next 15 years or so, you must not let it sleep on your bed as a kitten. Train it to stay indoors at night, in a room of your choosing, by closing it in the room with a comfortable bed, its evening meal, a water bowl and a litter tray. Having ensured it is comfortable and safe, ignore any indignant miaows.

Many owners worry that their cats will stop loving them if they lay down rules but the opposite is the case. Cats living in a feral group, for example, know there is a dominant cat which lays down rules. If they transgress those rules, they will be hissed at and maybe slashed at or bitten. So cats accept the idea of a dominant, boss cat – and, in your household, the boss cat should be you.

What if you want to teach your cat some tricks? Your success may depend to some extent on the colour of your cat, because professional trainers find ginger cats, tabbies and white cats the easiest to train. Black cats are almost impossible! Adult cats which have not been neutered are also almost impossible to train.

Start by buying some of your cat's favourite treats, which should be given at training sessions and at no other time. Hold the training session at the same time each day, every day. Choose a time when your cat is active, not just before or after a meal and not at nap time. Start with something very simple, like training your cat to come when its name is called. Call its name, rattle the treats and reward your cat with one every time it responds. As your cat learns each simple trick, you can go on to something more difficult, teaching it to sit or lie down on command, or jump through a hoop, or whatever. Each time it does what it has been asked to do, it should be rewarded with a treat.

Keep the training sessions short, no more than ten minutes. This is about the limit of a cat's attention span. After that it will become bored and a bored cat will do nothing it's told.

transfer of ownership

When you buy a pedigree kitten you will receive a transfer of ownership certificate which transfers the kitten from the breeder to you. The breeder should have filled in her/his section, you then fill in your section and send it to the appropriate registration body with the small fee which is charged for this service.

travelling

Travelling with a cat is always much easier if you have the cat in a secure carrier. It is essential if you are travelling by car. If a cat dives under the driver's feet, it could cause a very serious accident. Cardboard boxes are not suitable containers as a scared cat can rip its way out of one very quickly or, if a nervous cat urinates in it, the bottom of the box will disintegrate.

Some cats suffer from travel sickness and should not be fed before a journey. Others will insist on their regular meal before travelling, with no ill effects. Deprived of a meal, they will yell their heads off for the duration of

Turkish Van kittens

the journey. The cat carrier should be lined with something warm and comfortable for your cat's journey. If you fear it might be sick or urinate, line the carrier with a baby's disposable nappy or newspaper.

A sprinkle of catnip in the carrier might help your cat settle down. The driver should be asked to drive smoothly, especially around corners, so that the cat is not tossed from side to side. Pack your cat's food, bowl and water dishes, as well as its litter tray, if the journey is likely to be long. Remember if you have a rest stop, *do not* leave your cat shut in the car in sunlight. This can lead to **heat stroke**.

If you are **moving house**, some removal firms will now arrange the 'removal' of your pets too. There are also a number of specialist firms which can make travel arrangements for your pets whether the journey is a few miles or right across the globe. If taking your cat abroad, these companies can provide an invaluable service, as the rules and regulations on moving animals from one country to another can be extremely complex. More than one do-it-yourselfer has taken a pet abroad only to be refused entry to a country because the pet's paperwork was incorrectly completed.

Turkish Van   *(see above)*

The first Turkish Vans to be imported to the United Kingdom came from the Lake Van area of south-eastern Turkey. Perhaps their lakeside origins explain their love of water – they positively revel in it, enjoying swimming and splashing around in sinks and baths. They are known as the swimming cats.

They are full of character and independence. Although they do enjoy attention and fussing, they are very accommodating cats and will fit in well in any family situation. Think twice about a Turkish Van though if you have a pet bird. They retain many of their original characteristics and, as they were farm cats, they are good hunters. They should get plenty of exercise or otherwise they may become podgy.

They chatter to their owners and are determined and demonstrative cats. They are also attracted to bright things and small toys – which they may purloin – and will retrieve balls thrown by their owners.

According to the time of year, they can have two distinct coats and their winter coat can be enormous. Daily grooming – though it need only be brief – is necessary and shedding in spring can be quite heavy. The red markings over the Turkish Van's eyes are said to be the thumb-prints of Allah.

type, typey

Type is a word often heard among pedigree breeders and show people. It refers to a cat's appearance; if it conforms closely to the **standard of points** for the breed the cat will be said to be of good type – or typey.

U

UKFR

United Kingdom Feline Register – a registration organisation which also dispenses cat care information but does not perform any of the major functions of the **GCCF** or **CA** apart from registration.

undercoat

Under the fur 'topcoat' possessed by most breeds is a short and woolly undercoat of down hairs which helps trap air and keep the cat warm. The **Rex** has no topcoat, only an undercoat. Some silky-haired breeds, such as the **Ragdoll**, have only a topcoat and no undercoat.

undershot jaw

A mouth deformity where the lower jaw protrudes more than the upper, resulting in the teeth being unable to meet correctly.

upper respiratory disease

See **Feline Respiratory Disease**.

urine sample

A urine sample from your cat is required for diagnosis in a variety of conditions and this is quite easily obtained – once you know how. Don't wait behind your cat holding a small container; you could wait for ever.

Wash out the litter tray and fill it with shredded paper towels. When your cat urinates in the tray, you can squeeze the liquid out of the paper towels into a container. Or fill the tray with washed, smooth gravel. When the cat urinates, the urine will drain to the bottom and can be poured out.

Don't do what one owner did. When her vet asked her for a sample of her cat's 'water' she brought in a bottle which she had filled from her tap.

V

vaccinations

See **inoculations**.

vegetables

Many cats enjoy a small amount of chopped, cooked vegetables added to their diet. Although cats are carnivores, in the wild they would eat virtually all of their prey and this would include vegetable matter in the stomach. A meal with vegetables added to it should consist of at least two-thirds meaty food, with one-third (or less) vegetables. Ideally vegetables should not form such a large proportion of the diet.

Cats cannot remain healthy on an entirely vegetarian diet, being unable to synthesise many of their nutritional requirements from vegetable sources. A vegetarian cat would be deficient in vitamins A and B_3, essential fatty acids, **taurine** and, possibly, protein. The lack of taurine, a substance similar to an amino acid, would have the most dramatic effect. A lack of taurine can, over a period of years, lead to progressive retinal atrophy and irreversible blindness.

vets

The time to choose a vet is before you need one; not when you need one in an emergency. If you don't already have a vet ask friends and neighbours if they can recommend a vet who is good with cats. Some vets are better with dogs or horses than they are with cats, so it is best to ask the advice of cat lovers. Compare surgery hours and find out what facilities are available in case of emergency. Don't just choose the nearest vet or the cheapest vet; choose one you believe will look after your cat well, and one who has a good back-up service. If you have an automatic-dial telephone, place your vet's number on memory so you can contact him or her quickly in an emergency.

Vets do more than cure sick animals and provide preventive medicine. They also sell much of the equipment you will need for your pet, such as cat litter, flea sprays, disinfectants, even food. They are an excellent source of advice and local knowledge on everything to do with animals.

On the whole their charges are very reasonable. They carry out procedures on pets which, if carried out on humans and charged for, would cost several times as much.

See your vet if you are at all concerned about your pet's health. It is particularly important to take veterinary advice where cats are concerned because they are such stoic creatures they can be seriously ill before you notice that anything is wrong. Don't worry that you might be bothering your vet unnecessarily – it is far better to do that than lose a cat because you didn't consult your vet quickly enough.

vitamin supplements

Manufactured cat foods which state they are 'complete' contain all the vitamins and minerals required by the average adult cat. Supplements are usually only given to kittens, pregnant and nursing queens and elderly cats. Vitamin and mineral supplements for cats are available from veterinary surgeries and pet stores. Follow the recommended dosage carefully as overdosage can be dangerous.

vomiting

There are many reasons why a cat might vomit. The most common is the expulsion of a **hairball**, which may be accompanied by a coughing, honking sound. If it has eaten **grass**, this will irritate the stomach and make the cat vomit. Intestinal worms will make a cat vomit as will anything toxic or irritating which it may have eaten. A cat which eats too fast or too much may be sick afterwards. In this case feed it smaller meals more often. Or it might have a reaction against some of the additives in the food you are giving it; try another brand.

Vomiting can also be a symptom in a number of very serious illnesses so see your vet if:

▷ the vomiting is persistent
▷ there is blood in the vomit
▷ there is persistent diarrhoea as well
▷ your cat is listless and obviously unwell.

water

Forget milk – it is water that is vitally important for your cat's health. A bowl of clean water should be available at all times, even if you never see your cat drinking from it. See **drinks**.

wax

See **ears**.

weaning

Kittens, like most mammals, adore their mother's milk and would continue to feed from her as long as they are allowed to. Cats, however, will become debilitated if they feed their kittens for too long, so it is up to their human owner to persuade the kittens to start eating solid foods. Kittens mature at different rates and you will find that moggy kittens will be ready for weaning (eating solid foods) at the age of three to four weeks, while pedigree kittens, which mature more slowly, won't be ready for weaning until at least four weeks. Some slower pedigree breeds will have to be encouraged to wean at five weeks.

Young kittens should be fed four times a day. Start feeding them milky meals, using milk substitute (from your pet store or vet) mixed with baby cereal for bulk. Check packets to ensure the baby cereal contains little or no preservative or colouring. These meals can be alternated with meaty canned food. Several manufacturers now make specific foods for kittens, higher in protein and other nutrients than cat foods. Choose one which is as 'natural' as possible, or feed your kittens a tinned meaty baby food.

At five or six weeks of age, depending on the kittens' maturity, introduce cat food which you have chopped up, or mashed cooked fish.

At eight weeks, kittens are usually fully weaned. They are still eating four meals a day, which can be reduced to three at the age of four months and to two at six months.

wedge

The triangular head shape found in some breeds of cat, of which the Siamese is best known. The wedge 'starts at the nose and flares out in straight lines to the tips of the ears forming a triangle, with no break at the whiskers' according to the standard of points.

weight

According to the *Guinness Book of Pet Records* the average weight of a mature male cat is 6lb 2oz (2.81kg), while the average weight of a mature female is 5lb 4oz (2.45kg). The Ragdoll appears to win the highest average weight award with up to 20lb (9.07kg) recorded for the male and up to 15lb (6.8kg) for the female. The smallest breed may be the Singapura at 6lb (2.7kg) for the male and 4lb

(1.8kg) for the female. The heaviest domestic cat ever recorded was an Australian male weighing 45lb 10oz (20.7kg) at the age of 6½ years. Said to be a 'moderate' eater, he was possibly the victim of a hypothyroid condition.

whip tail

A tail which is long and thin and tapers to a fine point, such as that seen on the Siamese. Foreign-type cats have much thinner and longer tails than other types of cat.

whiskers

Whiskers, more correctly termed *vibrissae*, are the cat's sensors, as well as an indicator of its mood. Whiskers will be pushed forward in pleasurable anticipation or drawn back in a snarl. It is believed they help a cat find its way across rough ground at night and that they enable a cat to gauge the width of its body; if the whiskers won't fit through a gap, the cat believes its body won't fit. Certainly, long-haired cats have longer whiskers than short-haired cats.

Mother cats keep control of their most obstreperous kittens by chewing off their whiskers at an early age. Without the information gained from the whiskers, a kitten is slightly off balance and is slowed down sufficiently to be less bother to its mother.

Wood's lamp

If a cat is suspected of **ringworm**, a Wood's lamp will be used by your veterinary surgeon to light up its fur with ultra-violet light. Any ringworm present will fluoresce, as will any fluff on your clothes!

worms

Signs of worm infestation include diarrhoea or vomiting, constipation, weight loss, lack of interest in food, poor condition and pot bellies, especially in kittens.

Kittens will be born infected with worms and also become infected via their mother's milk, whether their mother was wormed or not. A severe infestation of worms can threaten a kitten's life if untreated as a mass of worms can block the intestines. Cats become infected by eating prey whose bodies contain encysted larvae, which develop into worms if eaten by a cat. If a cat swallows a flea with worm eggs in its system, these can also develop in the cat's body.

Worming preparations are available from pet stores and from veterinary surgeries. Instructions should be followed as overdosage can be dangerous, especially to kittens, and worming preparations should never be given within several days of flea treatments as, together, the two treatments can prove toxic. Always give cats worming preparations formulated for cats, not for dogs.

There are several different types of worm and they require different products for their treatment.

▷ *Roundworms*. The most common type of worm, they are found in the intestinal canal where they may prevent the proper absorption of food. They are much more serious in kittens than in adult cats. The worms are cylindrical and can be 4in (10cm) long although some even longer than this have been found.

▷ *Tapeworms*. These have segmented bodies which can be up to a metre in length. Some of the segments may break off and be visible around the cat's bottom. They look like brownish grains of rice and may still be wriggling when seen. As well as treating your cat for tapeworms, burn its bedding which may be harbouring the worm segments. It is important to keep your cat flea-free as fleas can cause re-infestation.

▷ *Heartworms*. As their name suggests, heartworms live in a cat's heart and blood vessels. Infection is not common but is sometimes found in hot countries where it is spread by mosquitoes. Symptoms can include a persistent cough, listlessness and loss of weight. Fluid may build up in the abdomen and there may be a change in the shape of the heart, which can be seen with X-rays. Veterinary treatment is essential and may involve injection with a drug to kill the heartworms, or surgery to remove them.

▷ *Hookworms*. These are a small, blood-sucking type of roundworm which can damage the intestinal lining. Hookworms start their journey to the intestines by burrowing into the skin when larvae. This may cause dermatitis. Other signs of these worms are diarrhoea, loss of weight and poor condition.

▷ *Lungworms*. Lungworms occur when cats eat prey with larvae in their bodies. Coughing, the main symptom, occurs when the lungworms move around the lungs. Although a cat may cough less in the later stages of the infestation, the cough will sound deeper. A cat may also sneeze and have diarrhoea. Veterinary attention is necessary.

▷ *Whipworms* and *threadworms*. Smaller than roundworms, these are bloodsuckers. Whipworms will be found in the large intestine and threadworms in the small one.

If in any doubt, always consult your veterinary surgeon about worm infestations.

Z

zoonoses

Zoonoses are diseases that can be transmitted from animals to humans. Included in the diseases which can be transmitted from cats to humans are **cat scratch fever**, **toxoplasmosis**, **rabies**, **ringworm** and infestation with the larvae of intestinal **worms**.